Twisted Cakes

DELICIOUSLY EVIL DESIGNS FOR EVERY OCCASION

Debbie Goard

PHOTOGRAPHY BY
BRUCE FLEMING

PROCESS PHOTOGRAPHY BY
CHRIS HIRNEISEN

HARPER
DESIGN

An Imprint of HarperCollins Publishers

To Chris, thank you for all your tireless work and never ending support. Without you none of this would be possible. You are the straight line to my squiggle.

Published in 2012 by:
Harper Design
An Imprint of HarperCollins*Publishers*
10 East 53rd Street
New York, NY 10022
Tel (212) 207-7000
harperdesign@harpercollins.com
www.harpercollins.com

First published in the UK in 2012 by:
Fil Rouge Press
110 Seddon House
London EC2Y 8BX

Distributed throughout most of the world by:
HarperCollins*Publishers*
10 East 53rd Street
New York, NY 10022

Library of Congress Control Number: 2012936931
ISBN: 978-0-06213404-2

Printed in China by Imago, 2012

Publisher: Judith More
Managing Editor: Jennifer Latham
Editor: Cécile Landau
Design: Gaye Allen

WARNING: Some cakes include non-edible items such as dowels, wire, and Styrofoam or monofilament in their structure or design. Please take care when cutting the cake and do not include non-edible parts when serving.

contents

Introduction

For as long as I can recall, I've been artistic. I'd draw on anything handy, even paper towels, and after years of honing my napkin-art skills, I hoped to parlay them into a career. I became an "artist for hire," doing everything from portraits to murals, but knew I'd need steady work, lest I literally starve!

My brother-in-law pulled strings to get me a job in a local market. There, I sliced lunch meats and learned the subtle differences between thin-sliced and shaved. This may not have been much improvement over my napkin-art era, but all the while I was also pursuing my creative endeavors. One day, hearing about my artistic leanings, my boss asked if I would take over from the retiring cake decorator. I had only made one cake in my life, but I was willing to learn. Within a week, I had made—and sold—my first professional offering.

Years passed, and my unexpected career continued, despite numerous attempts to escape. Then, in 2004, I decided to fully embrace the medium—but on my terms. I launched my own business in 2005, submitting my website (www.debbiedoescakes.net) for promotion to a pioneer in the field. She loved my work, but advised, "remove the dead-rat cake." With this, I knew I was on to something, and have continued to embrace subjects others warn against, creating a niche for myself—"twisted cakes." In this book, let me share with you my offbeat celebration of the weird, wacky, and wonderful.

Debbie Goard

Essential tools

BAKING TOOLS

An assemblage of tools used to bake cakes and create structures

1 SHEET AND ROUND PANS
2 VINYL WRAP for covering boards
3 MINIBALL PAN / CUPCAKE PAN
4 MEASURING CUP
5 FLOWER POT for baking flowerpot-shaped cake
6 SPORTS BALL PAN for baking sphere shapes
7 SIFTER
8 HOT-GLUE GUN used to attach ribbon
9 CUPCAKE LINERS
10 DRILL for attaching screws
11 COPPER TUBING for creating ax handle, etc.
12 PLIERS for bending copper
13 SIDE CUTTERS for cutting copper
14 WOOD SCREWS AND SCREWDRIVER used to secure dowels to board
15 DOWELS used as supports
16 WOOD BOARD used as a base for cakes that require screws/dowels

DECORATING TOOLS

A collection of traditional and unconventional tools used to decorate and complete the cakes.

1 LIGHT BOX for tracing
2 CRÈME BRULÉE TORCH for scorching and searing
3 SCALE
4 AIRBRUSH / COMPRESSOR to color cakes
5 FONDANT SMOOTHER
6 STYROFOAM BALL to create lightweight, inedible shapes
7 BURLAP for adding texture on icing
8 PAINTBRUSHES
9 MODELING TOOLS to add detail
10 CRAFT KNIFE
11 ROTARY FONDANT CUTTER a cutting wheel to cut even fondant strips
12 LARGE ROLLING PIN to roll out larger amounts of fondant
13 COFFEE STIRRERS to add detail
14 RULER
15 AIRBRUSH COLORS specially formulated colors to be used in the airbrush
16 LUSTER AND DISCO DUSTS edible dusts for adding sparkle and sheen
17 CMC to add firmness to fondant. When added to sugarpaste, it acts as a quick-drying, synthetic form of gum tragacanth, ideal for modeling paste.
18 SILVER HIGHLIGHTER to create shiny, metallic paint
19 GEL COLOR edible color for tinting and painting fondant
20 PALETTE to mix colors
21 SMALL ROLLING PIN
22 SCISSORS
23 SCRUB BRUSH to add textures
24 WAVY KNIFE to cut fondant fries
25 SERRATED KNIFE
26 SPATULA
27 MONOFILAMENT to make whiskers
28 LINED VINYL used as an impression mat
29 WAFER PAPER edible paper for logos, signs, etc.
30 METAL MESH for adding texture
31 TOOTHPICKS to secure fondant pieces
32 WIRE for antennae
33 FLOWER VEINER to add detail on gelatin pieces
34 GLOVES for mixing colors
35 PARCHMENT TRIANGLES to create icing bags
36 FLORAL WIRE to create legs, stems, etc.
37 WIRE CUTTERS for cutting wires
38 EDIBLE MARKERS used to draw logos, add detail, etc.
39 LARGE ICING BAG / QUICK ICE TIP
40 BENCH SCRAPER to smooth icing
41 DECORATING TIPS nozzles used to pipe icing/cut shapes
42 SQUARE CUTTER
43 ROUND CUTTER SET
44 PLASTIC CUPS to hold colors and glazes
45 CURVED SPATULA, SMALL OFFSET SPATULA, SMALL SERRATED KNIFE for icing curved surfaces
46 MEASURING SPOONS

Basic recipes

MODELING CHOCOLATE

YIELDS 3 CUPS (700 ML)

12 oz. (340 g) chocolate candy
   discs or coating chocolate
1/3 cup (75 ml) light corn syrup

- *glass bowl*
- *microwave*
- *spatula*
- *parchment or waxed paper*

Place chocolate in glass bowl. Microwave for about 45 seconds, stir with spatula, then return to microwave for an additional 45 seconds or less (time will vary, based on microwave model; be careful not to burn chocolate). Remove from microwave. Add corn syrup, stirring mixture with spatula until well blended. Do not overmix. Turn out and spread mixture onto waxed paper or parchment, then cover. For best results, let set overnight.

GANACHE

YIELDS 2 CUPS (470 ML)

8 oz. (225 g) semisweet
   chocolate, chopped or chips
1¾ cups (400 ml) heavy
   whipping cream
1 teaspoon pure vanilla extract

- *glass bowl*
- *small saucepan*
- *spatula*

Place chocolate in glass bowl. Set aside. Pour heavy whipping cream into saucepan, set over medium high heat. Stirring often, bring cream to a boil. Remove cream from heat and pour over chocolate. Stir with spatula until chocolate is fully melted. Mixture will be smooth and glossy. Stir in vanilla extract. Leave to set at room temperature for about an hour, or refrigerate for about 30 minutes until mixture is a spreadable consistency.

CREAM CHEESE ICING

YIELDS 3 CUPS (700 ML)

8 oz. (225 g) cream cheese
4 tablespoons or ½ stick (55 g)
   unsalted butter
3 cups (450 g) confectioner's
   sugar, sifted
2 teaspoons pure vanilla extract

- *large bowl*
- *electric mixer*
- *spatula*

Set cream cheese and butter out in advance to let soften. Place cream cheese and butter in bowl and blend until creamy using electric mixer. Stop machine and scrape any mixture down from sides of bowl with spatula. Add and mix in sifted sugar, a little at a time, until all sugar is blended in. Add vanilla extract and mix until fluffy.

DECORATOR'S BUTTERCREAM ICING

YIELDS 4½ CUPS (1 LITRE)

2/3 cup (150 g) shortening
2/3 cup (150 g) unsalted butter
2 teaspoons clear vanilla extract
   (you may substitute
   regular vanilla extract,
   but icing will be off-white)
1 1/3 dashes salt
6½ cups (750 g) confectioner's
   sugar, sifted
3 tablespoons milk

- *large bowl*
- *electric mixer*

Place shortening and butter in bowl and blend together, using electric mixer. Blend in vanilla extract and salt. Add sugar, one cup at a time, beating on medium speed. Add milk slowly, then turn mixer to high speed and beat until fully blended.

GELATIN WINGS

YIELDS 1 LB. (450 G)

unflavored gelatin, 1 packet
water

- *glass bowl*
- *microwave*
- *brush*
- *veining sheet or
   impression mat*
- *scissors*

Mix 1 part gelatin to 2½ parts water in bowl (exact quantities depend on gelatin brand; some packets are larger than others). Warm in microwave for 30 seconds. Remove from microwave and let set for 5 minutes. Remove and discard layer of "scum" that has formed on top, then return to microwave and rewarm.

Brush warm mixture onto veining sheet or impression mat. Let set for up to 5 hours. When mixture is set, it will release itself from sheet. Once dry, you can cut set gelatin with scissors.

VANILLA CAKE

YIELDS 24 CUPCAKES OR
¼ SHEET CAKE OR 2 X 8 IN.
(5 X 20 CM) ROUND CAKES

3 cups (280 g) cake flour
3 teaspoons baking soda
1 cup (225 g) butter, softened
2 cups (450 g) sugar
3 eggs
1 cup (235 ml) milk
1 teaspoon pure vanilla extract

- *large bowl*
- *electric mixer*
- *spatula or large spoon*
- *24-hole cupcake pan or ¼ sheet pan or 2 x 8 in. (5 x 20 cm) round pans*
- *toothpick*

Sift flour and baking soda into large bowl. Set aside. Using electric mixer on medium speed, blend together butter and sugar. Beat in eggs, one at a time. Alternatively, beat in flour mix and milk until fully blended. Mix in vanilla. Spoon batter into paper-lined 24-hole cupcake pan or greased and parchment-lined ¼ sheet pan or 2 x 8 in. (5 x 20 cm) round pans. Bake at 350°F (180°C). Cupcakes bake for 20-25 minutes; sheet and round cakes for 40-45 minutes. Cake is done when toothpick

inserted in center comes out clean. Leave to cool fully on wire rack, before removing from pans.

RED VELVET CAKE

YIELDS 24 CUPCAKES OR
¼ SHEET CAKE OR 2 X 8 IN.
(5 X 20 CM) ROUND CAKES

2½ cups (236 g) cake flour
½ cup (55 g) cocoa powder
1 teaspoon baking soda
½ teaspoon salt
1 cup (225 g) butter, softened
2 cups (450 g) sugar
4 eggs
1 cup (235 ml) sour cream
½ cup (115 ml) milk
1 teaspoon red food color
2 teaspoons pure vanilla extract

- *large bowl*
- *electric mixer*
- *24-hole cupcake pan or ¼ sheet pan or 2 x 8 in. (5 x 20 cm) round pans*
- *toothpick*

Sift flour, cocoa powder, baking soda and salt into large bowl. Set aside. Beat butter and sugar with electric mixer on medium speed, until fluffy. Beat in eggs one at a time. Mix in sour cream, milk, food color, and vanilla extract. Slowly beat in flour mixture on low speed until fully blended. Do not overmix. Spoon batter into paper-lined 24-hole cupcake pan or parchment-lined and greased ¼ sheet pan or 2 x 8 in. (5 x 20 cm) round pans. Bake at 350°F (180°C). Cupcakes bake for 20-25 minutes; sheet and round cakes for 40-45 minutes. Toothpick inserted in center comes out clean when cake is done. Leave to cool fully

on wire rack, before removing from pans.

DEVIL'S FOOD CAKE

YIELDS 24 CUPCAKES OR
¼ SHEET CAKE OR 2 X 8 IN.
(5 X 20 CM) ROUND CAKES

¾ cups (85 g) cocoa powder
1⅓ cups (300 g) sugar
1¼ cups (290 ml) milk, scalded
2 cups (190 g) cake flour, sifted
1¼ teaspoons baking soda
1 teaspoon salt
⅔ cup (150 g) shortening
3 eggs
1¾ teaspoons pure vanilla extract

- *large bowl*
- *electric mixer*
- *24-hole cupcake pan or ¼ sheet pan or 2 x 8 in. (5 x 20 cm) round pans*
- *toothpick*

Sift cocoa and ⅓ cup sugar into large bowl, and stir into milk until fully blended. Set aside. Sift together remaining sugar, flour, baking soda, and salt into other bowl. Beat with shortening and half of cocoa mixture, using electric mixer at medium speed. Add eggs, vanilla, and remaining cocoa, and beat until fully blended. Spoon batter into paper-lined 24-hole cup-cake pan or parchment-lined and greased ¼ sheet pan or 2 x 8 in. (5 x 20 cm) round pans. Bake at 350°F (180°C). Cupcakes bake for 20-25 minutes; sheet and round cakes for 40-45 minutes. Toothpick inserted in center comes out clean when cake is done. Cool fully on wire rack, before removing from pans.

Essential techniques

ICING A CAKE

Chill cake until nearly frozen. Place on a thin cake board, fixing it in position with a few dabs of decorator's buttercream icing (see page 10). If cake is layered, sandwich layers together by piping icing over top of bottom layer and placing another layer on top. Repeat as necessary. Fill a large piping bag, fitted with a quick-ice tip, with more icing. Gently squeezing the bag, pipe strips of icing over the top and sides of cake to completely cover it. For a smooth finish, spread icing with a spatula, holding it flat against the top and sides of cake, while turning the cake, preferably on a turntable cake stand.

COLORING FONDANT

Dust work surface lightly with confectioner's sugar and spread out fondant on it. Make a well in center, add a few drops of gel color (you can also use airbrush color sparingly), and knead until color is blended in. Repeat for a darker color, adding just a little color at a time to reach desired shade. If fondant becomes sticky, knead in a little confectioner's sugar. Wrap fully in plastic wrap and store in airtight container.

ROLLING OUT FONDANT

Knead fondant until pliable. Place on work surface, dusted with either confectioner's sugar or corn starch (corn starch is best for humid climates, as it dries out fondant more quickly). Flatten fondant with hands, then roll out with a rolling pin to about ¼ in. (5 mm) thick. Lift fondant occasionally to ensure it is not sticking to surface (dust work surface with more sugar or corn starch if needed).

COVERING A CAKE WITH FONDANT

If you are working with a small amount of rolled-out fondant, you can use your hands to lift and drape it over the iced cake. Note that the icing on the cake should still be moist to the touch at this point or the fondant will not adhere. If the icing has dried out, either airbrush a mist of water or vodka over the surface of the iced cake, or lightly brush the icing with water before applying the fondant. When working with a large piece of fondant, it is best to roll it loosely around your rolling pin and unfurl it from the rolling pin onto the cake. Once the fondant is on the cake, quickly smooth the surface, using either your hands or icing smoothers. Use a sharp knife to trim away any excess fondant.

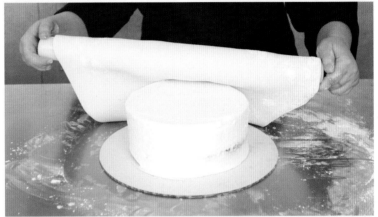
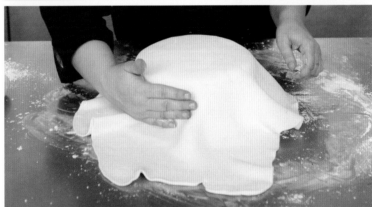

USING A TEMPLATE

Trace around the template with a pencil onto baking parchment. Cut out with scissors. Using dabs of buttercream icing, fix the cutout shape of parchment in position on the chilled cake. Cut around it, taking care to use a straight up and down motion to achieve a clean, vertical edge. Pull away excess cake and freeze it; you never know when you'll need a bit more cake. Remove the baking parchment shape.

SUPPORTING A TALL CAKE

Tall cakes need extra support. Cut cake into 4-6 in. (10-15 cm) high layers. Fix bottom layer to cake board with a few dabs of buttercream icing. Spread icing over top surface, dust with confectioner's sugar, and insert a few ⅛ in. (3 mm) dowels, cut to length, into the cake. Place thin piece of cake board, cut to shape, onto iced and doweled surface and stack next layer on top. Repeat until entire cake is stacked, then ice. With a very tall cake, use a wooden cake board and secure a length of ⅜ in. (8 mm) dowel to it—about 2 in. (5 cm) shorter than cake's full height. Drill pilot hole into the dowel and fix to board with a wood screw. Stack cake as above, with the addition of a hole cut in each layer of cake board to accommodate the length of ⅜ in (8 mm) dowel.

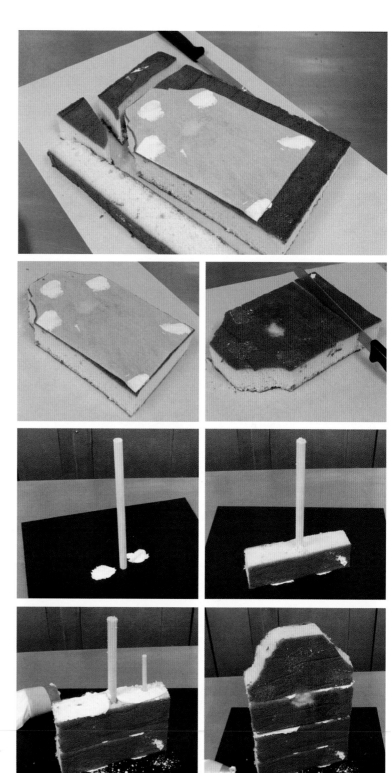

CARVING A CAKE

Cut chilled cake into layers and stack, using buttercream icing, as project requires. With a sharp, serrated knife and using a light sawing motion, carve away at cake, a little at a time. Go slowly until you have the desired shape; you can always carve off more later if needed, but it's difficult to add cake once it is cut away. Using a template or lightly sketching in guide marks into the cake with a small knife may help.

BUILDING DETAILS

Once your cake is carved and iced, but before you cover it with fondant, you may wish to build up details of features using modeling chocolate (see page 10). Think of the chocolate as the "clay" for your sculpture. Roll out "ropes" of modeling chocolate and shape them as instructed in the project that you are making, or as you feel is needed. Building features from chocolate is useful when you want to add details that are too delicate to carve directly from the cake itself. Another benefit of modeling chocolate is that it remains firm and maintains its shape under the weight of a fondant covering. Also, fondant adheres readily to modeling chocolate without needing any extra moisture. Once the cake is covered with a layer of fondant, you can use modeling tools to emphasize the details.

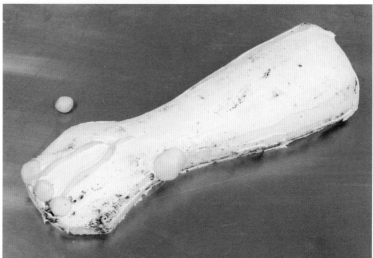

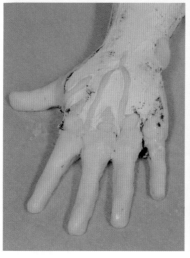 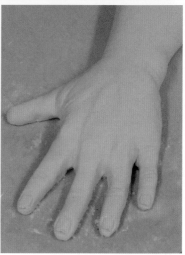

MAKING A PIPING BAG

A piping bag made from baking parchment is ideal when piping a small amount of icing or when you want to control the precise size of your icing tip. Cut out a triangle from baking parchment. Hold each end of the parchment between your thumb and forefinger, then turn one end over the thumb and forefinger holding the other end to start forming a cone. Point finger inside the cone toward the pointed end, and wrap over the opposite side to complete. Pinch the pointed end together to fix shape. Now fill the cone with icing, gel, or melted chocolate and crumple the top of it to create a bag. Snip off the tip of the pointed end to form a nozzle. This can be as small as you wish, but I advise cutting a smaller tip than you need, as it tends to stretch.

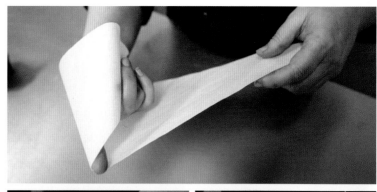

APPLYING PAINT AND PEARL DUST

Create a "paint" by mixing approximately one tsp. of luster, pearl, or highlighting dust with a few drops of vodka or lemon extract. Less is more when adding liquid to dusts; you can always add more if the paint is too thick. Stir mixture until fully blended. Brush on in even strokes. Leave to dry.

AIRBRUSHING

I prefer to use a double-action internal-mix airbrush that lets you switch colors without constantly changing cups. Use colors specially made for your airbrush, or mix your own from dusts and vodka, making sure they are thin enough to flow through the airbrush needle. Put a few drops of color in the airbrush and pull back the lever to start airflow. Test on paper before spraying cake. When you are happy, spray color onto cake in light, long strokes. Slowly build up light coats of color. Saturating your cake with a heavy coat causes pooling of moisture or pitting. Applying light layers builds up safely to rich, deep tones of color.

APPLYING LETTERING

Photocopy any lettering or logo for your project and tape the printout onto a light box or a well-lit window. Place a sheet of edible paper over the lighted image and, using light strokes, trace and color image onto edible paper with edible markers. Let dry, then cut out image with scissors. Apply a thin coat of piping gel to the back of cutout image and set in place on the cake. Smooth over with clean hands until fully adhered.

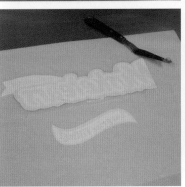

dead

tasty

What better way to celebrate an occasion than with a "memento mori"—a reminder of our own mortality? Whether it's a "Happy birthday, you SURE are getting OLD!" or a "Happy Halloween, let's remember the reason for the season," digging into a cake gravestone reminds us all to eat, drink, and be merry today, for we will be dead soon enough!

iced gravestone

stuff you'll need

- gravestone, skull and crossbones, and "R.I.P." templates
- baking parchment
- 12 in. (30 cm) square wooden cake board, ½ in. (1 cm) thick
- shelf paper (self-adhesive)
- 3 ft. (1 m) length ⅜ in. (8 mm) doweling
- drill
- no.6 wood screw
- serrated knife
- 2 ft. (0.6 m) length ⅛ in. (3 mm) doweling
- thin cake board
- large piping bag and quick-ice tip
- spatula
- rolling pin
- craft knife
- modeling tools, including ball tool
- scrub brush
- airbrush
- stiff paintbrush

food stuff you'll need

- 2 x recipe vanilla cake batter (see page 11), baked in ½ sheet pan
- 4½ cups (1 liter) decorator's buttercream icing (see page 10)
- confectioner's sugar
- 3½ lb. (1.5 kg) white fondant
- black and white airbrush colors
- 2 cups (225 g) crushed chocolate-colored cookie crumbs

STUFF YOU'LL NEED TO KNOW

◄ USING A TEMPLATE
see page 14

◄ SUPPORTING A TALL CAKE
see page 14

◄ ICING A CAKE
see page 12

◄ ROLLING OUT FONDANT
see page 13

◄ COVERING A CAKE WITH FONDANT
see page 13

◄ AIRBRUSHING
see page 17

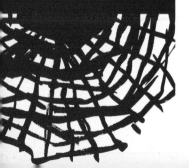

1 preparation

Use the gravestone template to cut out a gravestone-shaped piece of baking parchment. Cover cake board with self-adhesive shelf paper. Chill cake in freezer for 3-4 hours, until almost frozen, so it won't crumble when stacked.

2 create the support

Measure and cut a length of ⅜ in. (8 mm) doweling for the center support. It should be about 2 in. (5 cm) shorter than height of gravestone. On the reverse of the cake board, mark where center of the cake will rest. Drill pilot holes in the board and dowel. Screw dowel into cake board with no.6 wood screw.

3 cut out the cake

Place the baking parchment template on the firm, almost-frozen cake, fixing in place with a few dabs of decorator's buttercream icing. Using a serrated knife, cut out the gravestone shape from the cake.

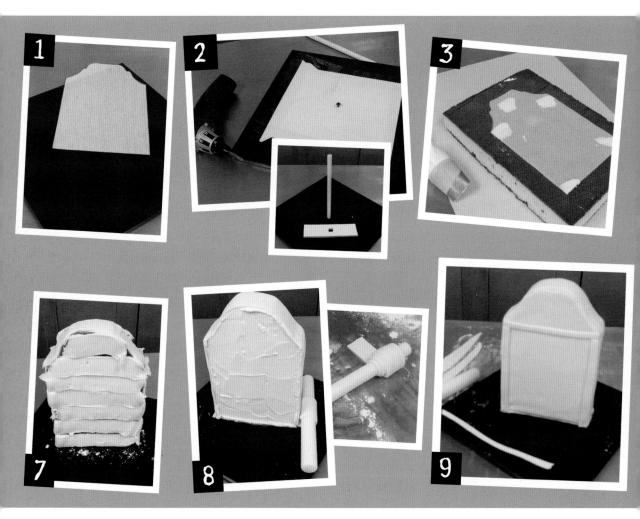

7 ice the cake

Using the large piping bag and quick-ice tip, apply buttercream icing over the entire cake in strips. Smooth over the iced surface with a spatula.

8 cover sides

Roll out white fondant and cut out a strip that is long and wide enough to cover the sides of the gravestone. Slowly roll fondant strip back onto your rolling pin, then unroll onto the sides of cake. Trim as necessary.

9 cover front and back

Cut front and back shapes of gravestone from rolled-out fondant using parchment template. As with sides, unfurl onto cake, smoothing with hands to fix in place. Cut thin strips of fondant for decorative trim. Attach with dab of water.

4 section the layers

With a serrated knife, cut horizontally across the lower part of the cake, dividing it into 2 in. (5 cm) wide sections and stopping below the shaped top. These will become the cake layers. Put two dabs of buttercream icing on either side of the dowel support on the cake board to secure the first layer.

5 stack the layers

Fix bottom layer of cake to board. Spread buttercream icing over top surface and dust lightly with confectioner's sugar. Cut two 6 in. (15 cm) lengths of ⅛ in. (3 mm) doweling and insert into either side of cake. Cut a piece of thin cake board to shape and place on top of iced surface.

6 complete stacking

Continue stacking the cake layers, fixing in place with buttercream icing and ⅛ in. (3 mm) dowels as described in Step 5 until all the layers are in place, including the shaped top.

10 add detailing

Roll out remaining fondant to about ¼-½ in. (.5-1 cm) thick. Using template, cut out skull and crossbones detail. Fix on gravestone with dabs of water. Add detail with modeling tools, creating cracks and imperfections. Imprint texture on surface with scrub brush.

11 add inscription

Trace "R.I.P." template onto baking parchment. Use as guide to imprint letters on stone by pressing with a ball tool. Airbrush black lightly over stone. Use stiff paintbrush to splash with black and white airbrush colors to create stippled effect.

12 add the soil

Pipe a mound of buttercream icing around base of the stone using piping bag and quick-ice tip. Press crushed cookie crumbs onto the icing until fully covered. With a stiff paintbrush, brush away any loose or unwanted soil.

For more than 3,000 years, the indigenous peoples of Mexico have held celebrations to honor the dead. Day of the Dead, or *Día de los Muertos* as it is known, is believed to be a time when the dead return for a visit, and it is celebrated from All Saints' Day to All Souls' Day (November 1 and 2). Intricately decorated skulls are symbols used to represent death and rebirth. This year, why not treat your "visitors" to a cake worth coming back from the dead for?

day of the dead

stuff you'll need

- paintbrushes
- 12 in. (30 cm) round cake board
- rolling pin
- craft knife and serrated knife
- stripe stencil
- airbrush
- black ribbon
- scissors
- hot-glue gun
- baking parchment
- 1½ in. (4 cm), ½ in. (1 cm) and ⅛ in. (3 mm) round cutters
- leaf, flower, and heart cutters
- large piping bag and quick-ice tip
- curved spatula

food stuff you'll need

- 3 lb. (1.3 kg.) white fondant
- black airbrush color
- 5 oz. (135 g) modeling chocolate (see page 10): 2 oz (55 g) tinted blue, 2 oz. (55 g) tinted pink, 1 oz. (25 g) tinted green, plus extra for details
- 1-2 oz. (25-55 g) each yellow, red, and pink fondant
- confectioner's glaze
- disco dusts: gold, red, and blue
- 2 x recipe red velvet cake batter (see page 11), baked in 3 x 8 in. (20 cm) round pans and half of 8 in. (20 cm) sports ball pan, chilled
- 4½ cups (1 liter) decorator's buttercream icing (see page 10)
- black gel color
- vodka or lemon extract
- ½ cup (110 g) chocolate discs, melted

STUFF YOU'LL NEED TO KNOW

◄ ROLLING OUT FONDANT
see page 13

◄ AIRBRUSHING
see page 17

◄ CARVING A CAKE
see page 15

◄ ICING A CAKE
see page 12

◄ COVERING A CAKE WITH FONDANT
see page 13

◄ APPLYING PAINT AND PEARL DUST
see page 16

◄ MAKING A PIPING BAG
see page 16

1 cover the board

Brush cake board surface with water to moisten. Roll out 1 lb. (450 g) white fondant and cut out circle about 14 in. (35 cm) in diameter. Drape over wet cake board. Smooth with hands. Trim away excess fondant.

2 add the stripes

Position a ready-made stripe stencil (see Resources, page 127) over the fondant-covered board. Airbrush over with several coats of black color. Carefully lift off the stencil.

3 finish the edges

Measure and cut a length of black ribbon to trim the edge of board. Attach in place with beads of hot glue. Set aside.

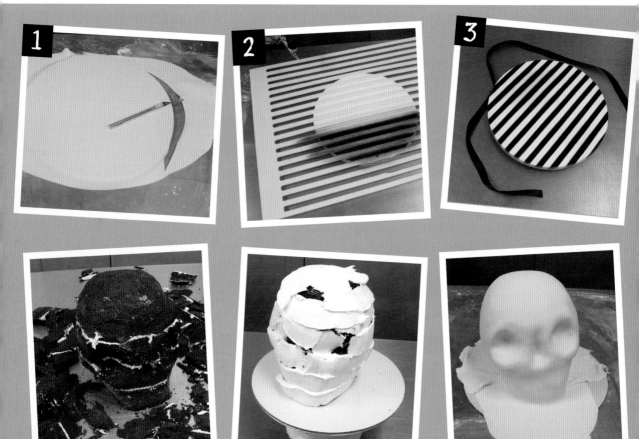

7 carve the cake

With serrated knife, carve the cake into a rough skull shape. Carve out the eye and nasal sockets. Shape and narrow in the cake around the jawline area.

8 ice the cake

Using large piping bag and quick-ice tip, cover the entire cake with buttercream icing. Smooth icing with a curved spatula. Use modeling chocolate to build up areas around the eye sockets for more prominent features.

9 cover the skull

Roll out remaining white fondant. Drape over the iced skull cake. Smooth fondant with your hands, paying special attention to the eye and nose area. Trim away excess.

4 make the roses

Roll out blue chocolate between two sheets of parchment. Cut out circle with 1½ in. (4 cm) cutter. Form into a cone. With ½ in. (1 cm) cutter, cut out petals and arrange, overlapping, around cone until desired size is achieved. Repeat with pink chocolate. Roll out green chocolate and cut out leaves. Leave all to set.

5 make the jewels

Roll out yellow, red, and pink fondant and cut out various shapes using the ⅛ in. (3 mm) leaf, flower, and heart cutters. Set pieces on parchment sheets, one for each color. Paint with a thin coat of confectioner's glaze. Sprinkle disco dusts onto still wet, glazed pieces. Leave to dry and set.

6 prepare the cake

Assemble the three round, chilled cake layers on top of each other, sandwiching them together with decorator's buttercream icing. Place the chilled half-ball cake layer on top with more buttercream. Shift assembled cake to arrange at a slant.

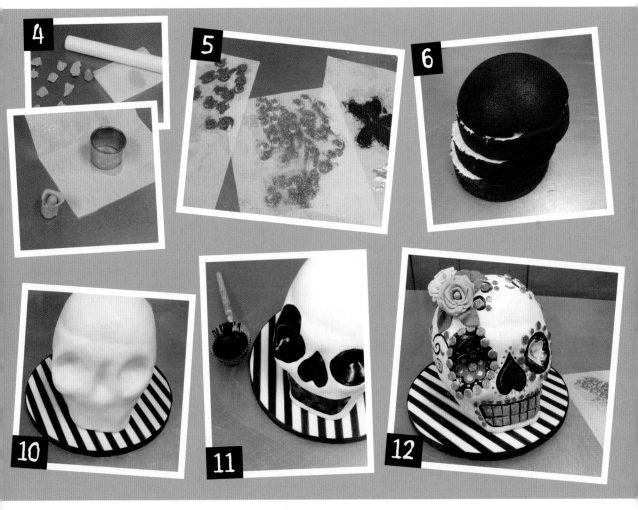

10 place skull in position

Place a dab of buttercream onto the prepared cake board. Carefully lift the fondant-covered skull cake and set it in place on the board. Tuck fondant edges under as necessary.

11 paint the skull

With a mixture of black gel color and vodka or lemon extract, paint the eye, nose, and mouth areas. Add decorative swirls and other flourishes as desired.

12 add the decor

Make small piping bag with baking parchment. Fill with melted chocolate discs. Snip end. Arrange the prepared jewels on cake, attaching each with a dot of piped chocolate. Fix roses and leaves in place with more piped chocolate.

The voodoo doll is derived from the English poppet, a doll used in folk magic and witchcraft to represent a specific person. It's said that actions performed on a poppet are transferred to that person. Lovesick? Sick of a loved one? Fashion a cake doll of your target, and insert pins. What better way to say, "I'm thinking of you"?

voodoo doll

stuff you'll need

- Styrofoam block, for drying pins
- paintbrushes
- small container
- rolling pin
- no.2A and no.6 icing tips
- craft and serrated knives
- baking parchment
- doll template
- large piping bag and quick-ice tip
- 12 in. (30 cm) square wooden cake board, ½ in. (1 cm) thick, covered with black self-adhesive shelf paper
- curved spatula
- fondant smoother
- stiff burlap
- modeling tool
- stitching wheel
- airbrush
- heart cutter

food stuff you'll need

- 6-8 thin spaghetti strands
- silver luster dust
- vodka or lemon extract
- 6 oz. (175 g) red fondant
- super pearl dust
- 2 oz. (55 g) black fondant
- 1 recipe devil's food cake (see page 11), baked 8 in. (20 cm) square pan and 2 holes of miniball pan
- 2½ cups (585 ml) decorator's buttercream icing (see page 10)
- 1 lb. (450 g) white fondant
- 4 oz. (110 g) modeling chocolate (see page 10)
- warm brown airbrush color

1 prepare the pins

Start making the pins at least a day ahead of presenting the cake. Break off small lengths of spaghetti, about 2–3 in. (5–7.5 cm) long, and carefully insert into the Styrofoam block so that they are held firmly upright.

2 paint the pins

Paint the spaghetti strands with silver luster dust mixed with a few drops of vodka or lemon extract. Place in Styrofoam block to dry.

3 form the pinheads

Pinch off small pieces of the red fondant and roll them into very small balls to create the pinheads.

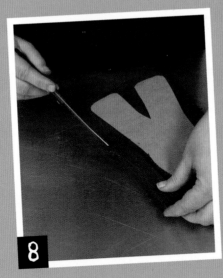

7 finish the buttons

With smaller end of no.2A icing tip, imprint rim detail on buttons. Using smaller end of no.6 icing tip, cut four holes in each button. Roll out more black fondant and use craft knife to cut thin strips for thread. Insert into buttonholes. Let dry.

8 cut out the cake

Cut out baking parchment shape using doll template. Attach parchment shape to chilled square cake with a few dabs of decorator's buttercream icing. Cut body shape from the cake, following the outline of the parchment shape.

9 shape the cake

With the serrated knife, shape the sides of the doll's body, slightly rounding the cake off at the edges.

4 position the pinheads

Place the fondant pinheads in a small container, a few at a time, and lightly sprinkle with dry pearl dust. Insert a pinhead carefully onto the top of each dry painted spaghetti strand. Leave overnight to set.

5 create button eyes

Roll out the black fondant on a lightly dusted surface to a thickness of about ½ in. (1 cm).

6 cut out buttons

Using the larger end of the no.2A icing tip, cut two round shapes from the rolled-out black fondant. Set aside the trimmings.

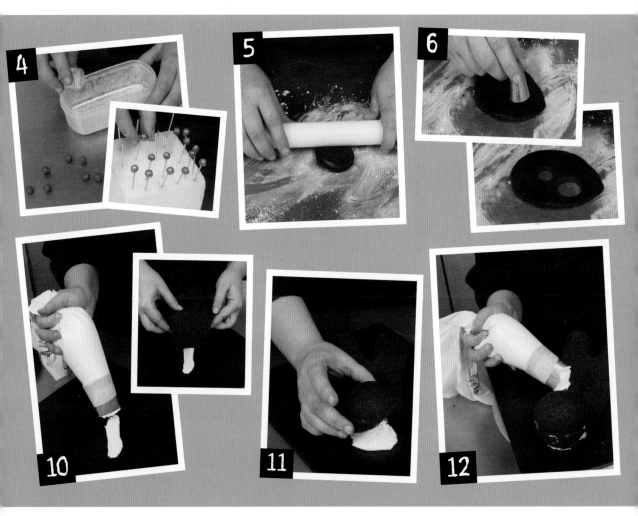

10 fix body to board

With large piping bag and quick-ice tip, pipe a strip of buttercream icing onto the covered cake board, and lay the body-shaped cake on top to fix in place.

11 make the head

Pipe a layer of buttercream over the flat surface of one mini half-ball of cake. Place the other mini half-ball of cake on top to form the doll's head.

12 attach the head

Place the cake head onto the body on the cake board using a dab of buttercream icing to fix it in place.

13 ice the doll

Pipe buttercream all around the outline of the head and body of the doll, then pipe more buttercream over entire top surface of doll until it is completely covered in icing.

14 smooth the icing

Using the curved spatula, carefully smooth over the entire surface of the icing, covering all of the doll.

15 prepare fondant cover

Roll out the white fondant onto a dusted surface. Using fondant smoother and stiff burlap, imprint surface of fondant with texture.

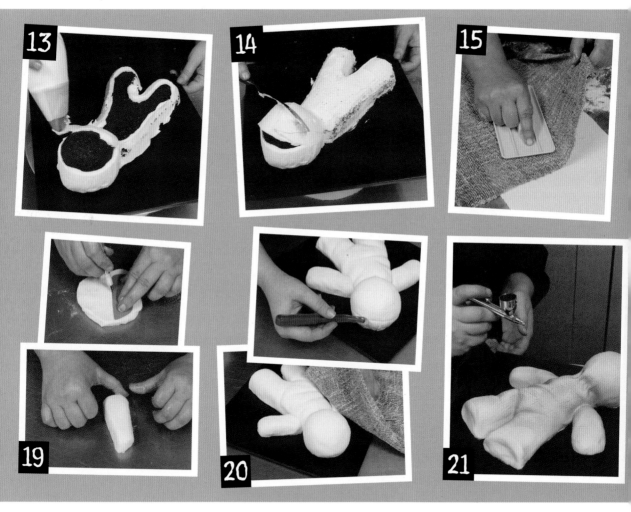

19 make the arms

Shape the arms from modeling chocolate. Roll out reserved white fondant and wrap around the chocolate arms. Trim away excess fondant.

20 attach and texture arms

Attach the arms to the body with a dab of water. Imprint the arms with burlap, as was done for the body in Step 15. With stitching wheel, add stitching detail all along the sides of the head and body.

21 airbrush the doll

Airbrush light layer of warm brown color all over the head and body, emphasizing the details and shape of features.

16 cover the doll

Carefully wrap the textured fondant loosely around rolling pin. Gently unfurl the fondant onto the iced doll, covering the body and head.

17 trim and shape body

Trim off excess fondant from around the doll with a craft knife and set aside. Tuck under edges of fondant on doll for a rounded look.

18 add features

Using modeling tool, mark outline of muscles and other anatomical details by adding folds to the body and legs of doll.

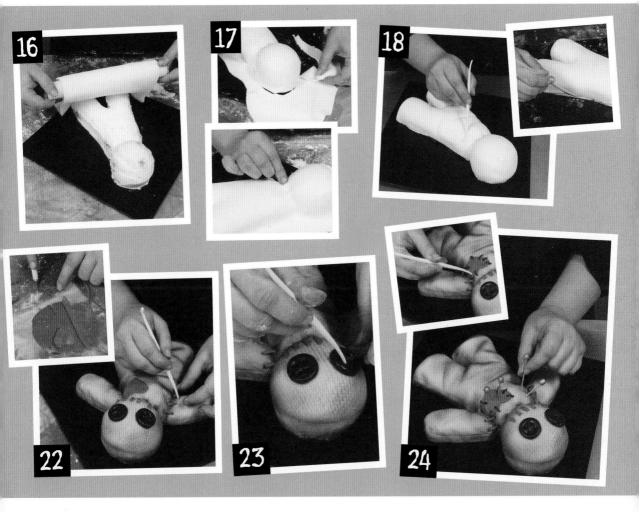

22 add heart and stitching

Roll out remaining red and black fondant. Cut voodoo heart template from red fondant with cutter. Fix to doll with dab of water. Indent holes at stitch sites on mouth, arms, neck, and heart. Cut thin strips of red and black fondant and insert ends into holes.

23 add button eyes

Position the prepared button eyes in place on the head and fix in place with a dab of water. Use modeling tool to emphasize the detailing on the eyes.

24 position the pins

Carefully remove the prepared pins from the Styrofoam block and insert into the body of the voodoo doll.

twisted
illusions

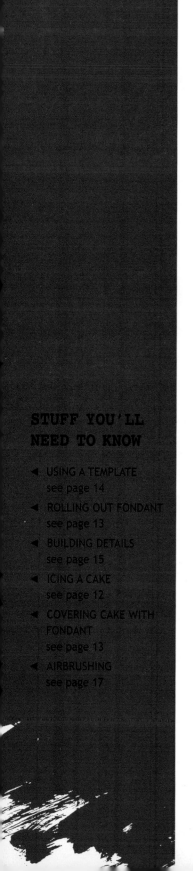

The term *Siamese* is derived from a famous pair of conjoined twins, Chang and Eng Bunker of Siam. They spent a decade exhibited as curiosities, then used their earnings to buy a plantation in North Carolina, where they lived out their days. Like the Bunkers, these piglets spend their days on the farm as happy as two pigs in chocolate mud can be.

siamese pigs

stuff you'll need

- pig belly and ear templates
- 6 x 10 in. (15 x 25 cm) plywood sheet, ¼ in. (5 mm) thick
- 6 x 10 in. (15 x 25 cm) Styrofoam sheet, 2 in. (5 cm) thick
- 3 ft. (1 m) lengths each: ½ in. (1 cm) and ¾ in. (2 cm) doweling
- shelf paper (self-adhesive)
- pen
- drill, with ³⁄₁₆ in. (5 mm) and ⅛ in. (3 mm) drill bits
- screwdriver
- no.8 drywall or wood screws
- hot-glue gun
- small serrated knife
- 16 in. (40 cm) round wooden cake board, ½ in. (1 cm) thick
- rolling pin
- craft knife
- toothpicks
- aluminum foil
- 2 x 1½ in. (4 cm) Styrofoam rounds; 2 x 3 in. (7.5 cm) Styrofoam balls
- ball tool
- large piping bag with quick-ice tip
- 2¾ in. (7 cm) round cutter
- spatula
- airbrush; stiff paintbrush

food stuff you'll need

- 1 tsp. CMC powder
- 2 lb. (900 g) light pink fondant; 3 oz. (85 g) black fondant
- 1½ lb. (675 g) modeling chocolate (see page 10)
- 1 recipe cake batter of choice (see page 11), baked in ¼ sheet pan
- 2 cups (470 ml) decorator's buttercream icing (see page 10)
- fleshtone airbrush color
- 2 cups (470 ml) ganache (see page 10)
- ½ cup (60 g) cookie crumbs

1 cut out the pieces

Cut separator board from plywood, and belly from Styrofoam. Cut ¾ in. (2 cm) dowel into 2 x 5 in. (13 cm) pieces; ends trimmed at 20° for left-side legs; a 4¾ in. (12 cm) piece, trimmed at 15° for right front leg; and a 4½ in. (11 cm) piece. Cut 2 x 5¼ in. (13 cm) lengths of ½ in. (1 cm) dowel, trimming one end of each at 20°, for neck pieces.

2 prepare the structure

Cover top of separator board with shelf paper. Place template on separator board. Use pen to mark position of screw holes to attach leg and neck dowels. Drill holes through board where marked, using ⅛ in. (3 mm) drill bit. Drill each end of leg dowels and angled ends of neck dowels, with ⅛ in. (3 mm) drill bit.

3 assemble neck and belly

Attach neck dowels to top of separator board, from underside, using screwdriver and no.8 drywall or wood screws. Rotate dowels so that they are angled to each side of separator board. Using hot-glue gun, attach belly Styrofoam to the underside of board.

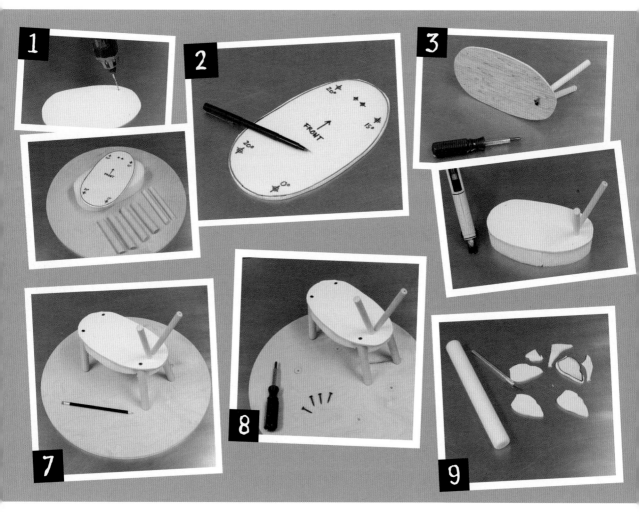

7 position structure on base

Place the structure on the 16 in. (40 cm) round wooden cake board. Position rear body of the pigs slightly off center of board to accommodate the heads. Mark the position of dowel ends, using pen.

8 attach structure to base

Drill holes through center of the marked dowel positions, using ³⁄₁₆ in. (5 mm) drill bit. Using the screwdriver and no.8 screws, attach the structure firmly to the base.

9 cut out the ears

Mix the teaspoon of CMC with 6 oz. (175 g) of light pink fondant. Roll out onto dusted surface to about ¼ in. (5 mm) thickness. Using the craft knife and the ear template cut out four ears from the rolled out fondant.

4 contour belly

Using small serrated knife, cut notches on each side of belly foam to accommodate all four leg dowels. With a sawing motion, use serrated knife to gradually round edges of foam. Narrow slightly at ends, to create a rounded belly.

5 attach the legs

Using screwdriver and no.8 screws, attach the legs to the underside of separator board. Angle left-side legs and the right front leg slightly forward.

6 adjust the legs

To create a more animated look, rotate the legs slightly outward.

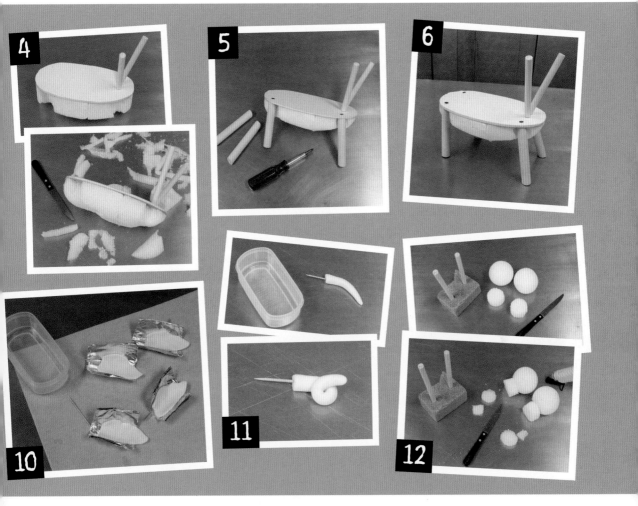

10 shape and dry ears

Insert moistened toothpicks into ends of the ears. Shape foil into thick squares to create formers. Round foil squares slightly. Place an ear onto each rounded foil shape. With the foil formers, curl edges of ears in to create folds. Leave to set.

11 form the tail

Using the remaining CMC and pink fondant mixture, roll out a small snake about 4 in. (10 cm) long. Narrow slightly at one end. Insert moistened toothpick into larger end. Curl fondant to create the tail. Let dry.

12 assemble heads

Place leftover dowels into scrap Styrofoam block to create a workstand. Using hot-glue gun, attach 1½ in. (4 cm) Styrofoam discs to 3 in. (7.5 cm) Styrofoam balls to make snouts. With serrated knife, trim at a slight downward angle.

13 shape foam balls

Using small serrated knife and ball tool, make recesses for eyes and nostrils. Carve away ball slightly to create jaw and chin areas. Trim bottom of snout to create flattened area.

14 build the head details

Using modeling chocolate, build up the features around the eye and snout area. Smooth a thin layer of modeling chocolate over entire heads to cover.

15 prepare to cover the heads

Using the rolling pin, roll out enough of the light pink fondant to cover the two heads.

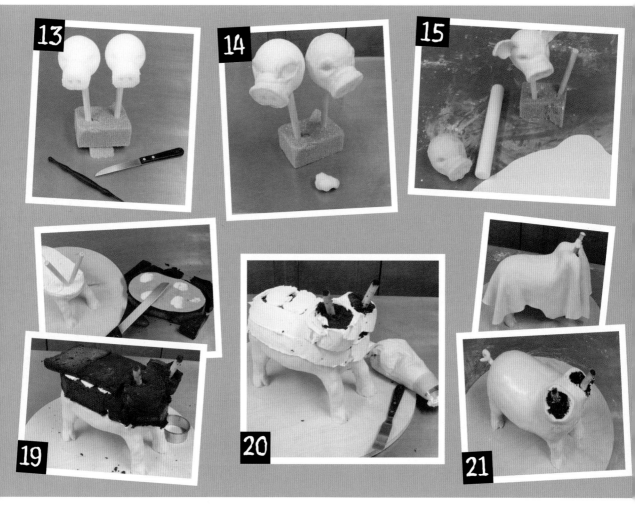

19 add the cake

Use template and serrated knife to cut two belly shapes from chilled cake. Place one on structure. Pipe over buttercream and stack second layer. Cut two rounds of cake using 2¾ in. (7 cm) cutter. Place over neck dowels.

20 ice the cake

Cover entire cake with buttercream, using large piping bag and quick-ice tip. There is no need to cover modeling chocolate as fondant will adhere to it without added icing. Smooth icing with a spatula.

21 cover body with fondant

Roll out remaining pink fondant. Drape over cake, smoothing quickly. Trim away fondant from top of neck areas. Smooth fondant with hands onto belly and legs, trimming as needed. Add detail to body and hooves with ball tool.

16 cover the heads

Drape pink fondant over chocolate-coated heads. Smooth with hands until well covered. Trim excess. Use ball tool to emphasize facial details, inserting ball tool into the eye and nostril recesses and forming the mouth opening.

17 position the ears

Poking with a moistened toothpick, mark out ear-position guideholes. Attach the dried ear pieces using water or a dab of melted chocolate. Set heads aside.

18 cover the structure

Cover leg and belly structure with modeling chocolate. A very light coat should suffice on the belly; only add more where extra roundness is desired. Build chocolate onto legs to thicken. Add thickness at hooves and knees. Build up and blend chocolate legs into belly area to create haunches.

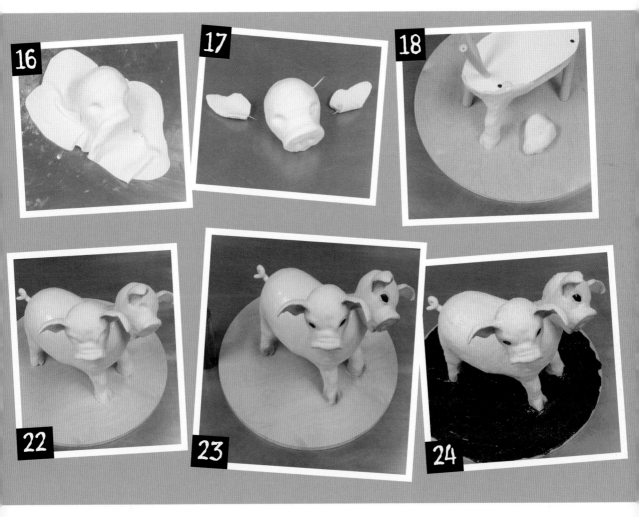

22 place parts on body

Place heads and tail onto covered body. Position heads as necessary to accommodate ears. Once heads are in desired position, attach with melted chocolate for added stability. Glue tail into place with melted chocolate.

23 add the details

Roll small balls of black fondant to form eyes. Insert into eye sockets using water to adhere. With ball tool, smooth eyes into shape. Spray a light coat of fleshtone airbrush color onto hooves, snout, and ear areas. Shade underbelly and leg creases lightly.

24 finish the cake

With stiff paintbrush, brush thin strokes of buttercream onto body to create hair. Move brush in direction of hair growth. Combine ganache and cookie crumbs to create thick "mud." Smooth onto the cake board with spatula.

In the puritanical seventeenth century, botanists found parallels between this carnivorous plant, which lures and digests its prey, and women, who were often portrayed as temptresses. Hence the plant was named after Venus, the goddess of love and power. Why not tempt your lover into your lair with sweet skills?

venus flytrap

stuff you'll need

- baking parchment
- 6 in. (15 cm) diameter clean new flowerpot
- spoon
- serrated and craft knives
- 6 pieces cloth-covered floral wire and wire cutters
- rolling pin
- plant head and stem templates
- half-ball or block of Styrofoam
- 10 in. (25 cm) square covered cake board
- large piping bag and quick-ice tip
- spatula
- airbrush
- modeling tool
- paintbrushes
- scissors
- 12-gauge green wire
- length of doweling or pencil

food stuff you'll need

- cocoa powder, for dusting
- ⅓ recipe cake batter of choice (see page 11)
- 8 oz. (225 g) modeling chocolate (see page 10), tinted light green
- 2 cups (470 ml) decorator's buttercream icing (see page 10)
- 1 lb. (450 g) fondant, tinted terra-cotta
- 1 cup (110 g) crushed Oreo cookies
- 2 oz. (55 g) black fondant
- emerald luster dust
- 1 lb. (450 g) gelatin wings (see page 10)
- green, pink, and red airbrush colors
- opaque white gel color

STUFF YOU'LL NEED TO KNOW

◀ ICING A CAKE
see page 12

◀ COLORING FONDANT
see page 12

◀ ROLLING OUT FONDANT
see page 13

◀ AIRBRUSHING
see page 17

◀ MAKING A PIPING BAG
see page 16

◀ APPLYING PAINT AND
PEARL DUST
see page 16

1 make the cake

Cut a circle of baking parchment to fit in the base of the flowerpot. Place in pot and dust sides of pot with cocoa. Spoon cake batter into pot and bake for 30-35 minutes, until toothpick comes out clean (see page 11). Let cake cool, then release from pot. Trim top to level with serrated knife. Chill in freezer.

2 cut out the plants

Twist two cloth-covered floral wires together to create one strong wire. Repeat for each plant. Roll out light green modeling chocolate to about ¼ in. (5 mm) thickness on a dusted surface. Using the templates, cut out two large plant heads, one small plant head, and three stems.

3 attach plants to wires

Press green chocolate stems and plant heads onto the prepared wires to create three plants, blending chocolate around wire to cover it. Trim away excess chocolate created by this process. Be sure to keep at least 3-4 in. (7.5-10 cm) wire exposed at the stem ends to insert into the cake.

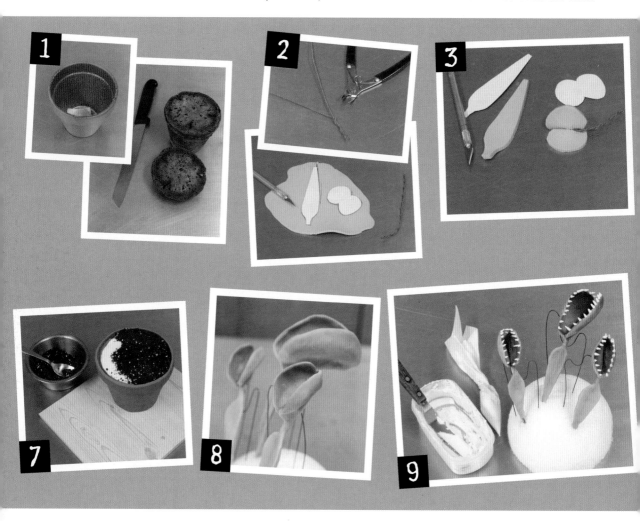

7 add the soil

Sprinkle a few spoonfuls of crushed Oreo cookies over top of the cake. A bit of the cookie filling is desirable in this crumb mixture, as it will resemble soil nutrients. Reserve remainder of crumbs.

8 airbrush the plants

Lightly spray light green shadows along the stems and plant-head mouths of the three prepared plants. Add a light coat of pink inside the mouths.

9 pipe the teeth

Make a small piping bag from baking parchment (see page 16) and fill with stiff buttercream icing (add a tsp. of cornstarch to buttercream to stiffen, if needed). Pipe teeth around the edge of plant mouths, using a squeeze and pull-away technique.

4 leave plants to set

Place the wired chocolate plants into a half ball or block of Styrofoam. Gently curve edges of stems and plant heads inward to create the mouth effect. If necessary, use wire crutches to support pieces. Allow to dry for about 2 hours, until set firm.

5 ice the cake

Put nearly frozen cake in position on the cake board, using a dab of buttercream icing to fix in place. Fill large piping bag, fitted with quick-ice tip, with more buttercream and use to cover entire cake with icing. Smooth surface of icing with a spatula.

6 cover the pot

Roll out terra-cotta fondant on a dusted surface. Cut out a rectangle, as long as the circumference and as wide as the height of cake. Wrap around sides of iced cake and trim as necessary. Cut a 1 in. (2.5 cm) wide strip of fondant, the length of cake circumference. Fix with water to top edge of pot. Trim to fit.

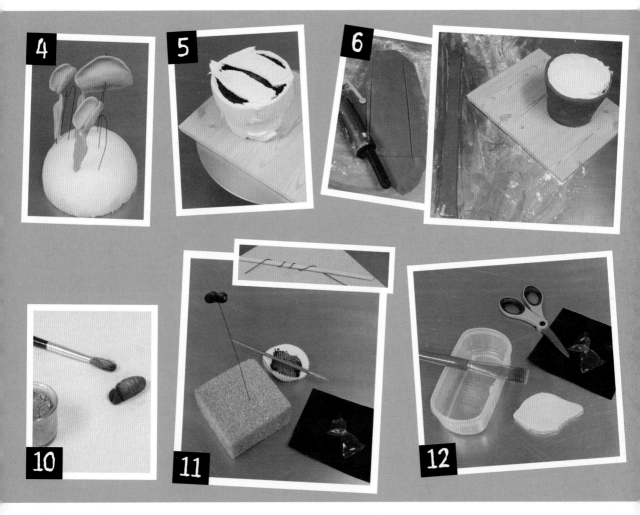

10 make the flies

Form black fondant into small, elongated balls, about 1 in. (2.5 cm) long. With modeling tool edge, imprint head segment. Roll out tiny balls of black fondant for eyes and attach with water. Dust fly bodies with emerald luster dust.

11 add details to the flies and shape fly wires

Place flies on lengths of wire to paint eyes with mix of red color and opaque white gel color. Let dry. Curl lengths of 12-gauge wire around a dowel or pencil. Make small loops at one end.

12 make wings and assemble

With scissors, cut out wings from prepared gelatin (see page 10). Press onto flies. Insert looped ends of wire into underside of flies, using water to fix. Insert prepared plants and flies into cake. Fill any spaces on the top surface of cake with Oreo crumbs and scatter over cake board.

There is something fun, and perhaps a bit devious, in serving a dish that deceives. Food illusion has a long history. The medieval dish "yrchouns"—a meatloaf with almond "spines"— was made to resemble a hedgehog, an animal widely eaten at the time. Some faux foods were produced as substitutes, as in the Civil War-era practice of grinding acorns to make "coffee." And sometimes food illusion was done for mere whimsy, as in the crafting of fruits from marzipan.

food fakery

stuff you'll need

- craft knife
- scrub brush
- large paintbrush or basting brush
- paper towel, moistened with vodka
- small plastic freezer bag
- ribs template
- thin cake board
- baking parchment
- serrated knife
- large piping bag and quick-ice tip
- small spatula
- rolling pin
- airbrush
- crème brûlée torch
- 14 in. (35 cm) oval platter
- bowl or jug
- wavy knife

food stuff you'll need

- 1 tbsp. CMC powder
- 1 lb. (450 g) ivory fondant
- airbrush colors: warm brown, ivory, chocolate brown, black, red
- 2-3 tbsp. flaked coconut
- green gel color
- 1 recipe vanilla cake batter (see page 11), baked in ¼ sheet pan
- 3 cups (700 ml) decorator's buttercream icing (see page 10)
- 2 lb. (900 g) white fondant
- 1 cup (235 ml) light corn syrup
- 1 tbsp. cornstarch
- black and white sanding sugars

STUFF YOU'LL NEED TO KNOW

◄ USING A TEMPLATE
see page 14

◄ CARVING A CAKE
see page 15

◄ ICING A CAKE
see page 12

◄ COVERING A CAKE
WITH FONDANT
see page 13

◄ AIRBRUSHING
see page 17

1 make the bones

Mix CMC powder into 4 oz. (110 g) ivory fondant. Roll into 7-8 snakes, each about 3 in. (7.5 cm) long, narrowing gradually at the ends, to form the bones. With craft knife, etch vertical lines into bones for cracks. Press scrub brush into large ends to create marrow effect. Let dry for at least 24 hours.

2 color the bones

Once bones have fully dried, brush a coat of warm brown color over entire surface. Using the paper towel, moistened with vodka, remove most of the color, allowing any color that has settled in the cracks and marrow to remain. Set bones aside to dry.

3 make the spices

Place the flaked coconut into the plastic freezer bag. Add a few drops of green gel color to the bag. Seal and shake until all the coconut is fully colored.

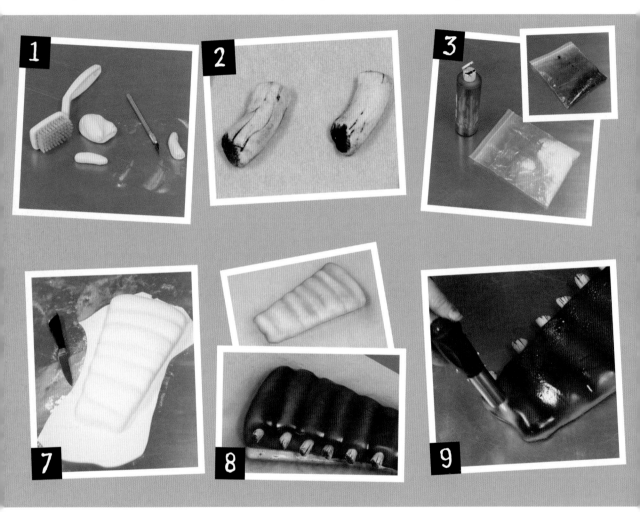

7 cover with fondant

Roll out the white fondant onto a dusted surface and drape it over the iced cake. Smooth the fondant carefully over the cake, emphasizing the rib sections.

8 airbrush the ribs

Airbrush on color in light coats, building tones for added realism. Start with a light coat of ivory, tracing over the rib sections. Next, airbrush even coats of warm brown, followed by chocolate brown and ending with touches of black.

9 torch the ribs

Place airbrushed cake on a nonflammable surface and use crème brûlée torch to "sear" random areas of the ribs to indicate scorch marks. Insert the dried bones. Place cake onto the oval platter.

4 cut cake board and parchment template

Use the template to cut out a ribs-shaped piece of thin cake board and a ribs-shaped piece of baking parchment. Place the parchment shape onto chilled or nearly frozen cake, fixing in place with dabs of buttercream icing.

5 carve the cake

With serrated knife, cut cake around parchment template. Place cut cake on ribs-shaped cake board, attaching with dabs of buttercream. Slice through entire length of cake, at an angle, from left to right. With a rounded motion, cut notches in top of cake, to form 7 or 8 ribs.

6 ice the cake

Fill large piping bag, fitted with quick-ice tip, with buttercream icing. Pipe icing over surface of cake, covering completely. Smooth over icing with small spatula, taking care to maintain the rib indentations.

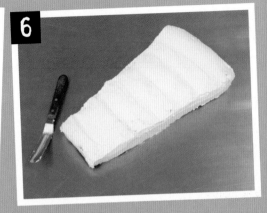

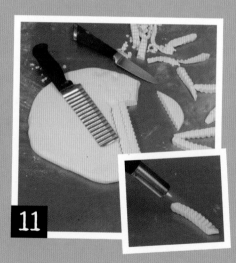

10 apply the sauce

In a bowl or jug, mix the corn syrup with the cornstarch, until blended. Add a few drops of red and warm brown airbrush color until desired sauce color is achieved. Brush mixture over ribs, allowing sauce to drip onto the bones.

11 make the fries

Roll out rest of ivory fondant on a dusted surface, to about ½ in. (1 cm) thick. Cut out fries with wavy knife. Trim all four sides of each fry to achieve the crinkled effect. Use crème brûlée torch on ends of the fries to give a crispy look.

12 arrange the platter

Place torched fries around ribs on platter. Sprinkle a mixture of black and white sanding sugars over ribs to resemble salt and pepper. Add pinches of the green-tinted coconut spices to season fries.

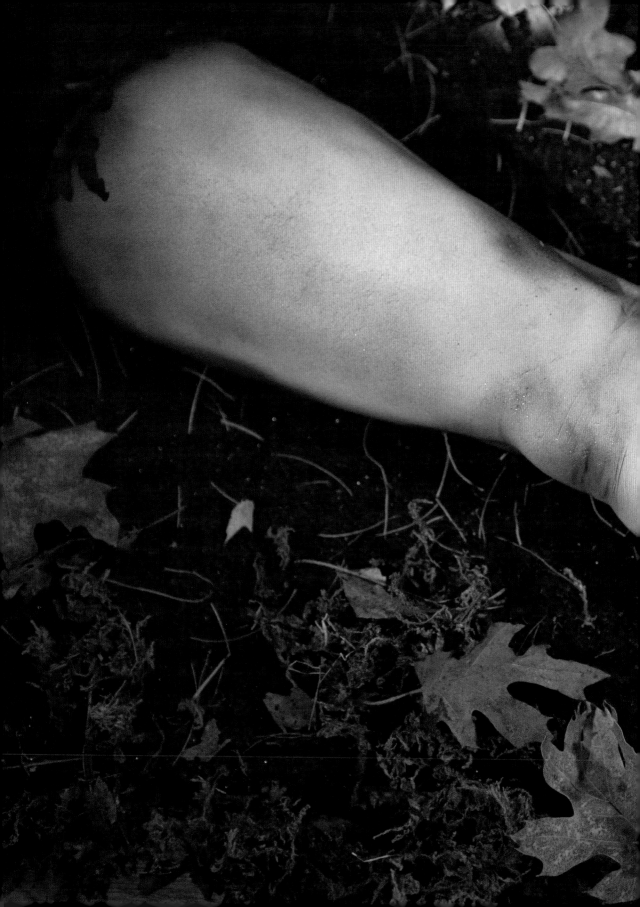

In my business, I have done a lot of cupcakes . . . I mean a LOT! After the 400th time you make something, you can start to go a bit mad. One day, in the midst of that madness, I felt a strange urge to stab something. In that moment it occurred to me, "Yes! I'll stab the cupcakes!" I set about crafting miniature knives. Surprisingly, tiny knives proved to be supercute. A trickle of sweet "blood" added the final touch. This exercise was very satisfying. The next time you feel the need to slash something, why not take a stab at these? Perfect for showers, or any get-together with the mother-in-law!

stabbed cupcakes

stuff you'll need

- small rolling pin
- knife template
- craft knife
- no.2 or no.3 icing tip
- coffee stirrer or flat implement
- cup, for mixing colors
- small paintbrush
- no.12 icing tip
- piping bag
- baking parchment
- scissors

food stuff you'll need

- 8 oz. (225 g) black fondant
- 2 tsp. CMC powder
- silver luster dust
- vodka or lemon extract
- 1 recipe red velvet cake batter (see page 11), baked in 24-hole cupcake pan lined with black cupcake cases
- 3 cups (700 ml) cream cheese icing (see page 10)
- ½ cup (115 ml) piping gel
- red food color
- 1 tsp. cornstarch (optional)

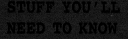

1 prepare the fondant
Place the black fondant on a lightly dusted surface. Sprinkle the CMC powder over it and knead until all the powder is evenly blended into the fondant.

2 roll out fondant
Using a small rolling pin, roll out the fondant mixture to a thickness of about ⅛ in. (3 mm).

3 cut out the knives
Use template to cut out knife shape from the fondant with a craft knife. Cut just a few knives at a time, as fondant tends to set quickly and you will want the knives to remain pliable when adding detail (Step 6).

7 start to ice the cupcakes
Arrange the cupcakes on a clean, flat surface. Fit the no.12 icing tip onto the piping bag, then fill the bag with the cream cheese icing. On top of each cupcake, pipe a swirl of icing, starting from the center.

8 finish icing
Work your way around each cupcake until well covered. You want a nice thick layer of icing. Finish with a swirly peak.

9 add the knives
Insert a fully set and painted knife into each of the iced cupcakes at a "just-stabbed" angle.

4 mark out the rivets

Using the small end of a no.2 or no.3 icing tip, indent three "rivets" along the handle of each knife.

5 sculpt the blades

With coffee stirrer or other flat implement, imprint a thinner, flatter area along edge of knife blades. Repeat Steps 3-5 until you have 24 knives. Let set and harden in cool place for 1-2 days.

6 paint the blades

Mix silver luster dust with a little vodka or lemon extract to form a thick liquid. With a small paintbrush, paint the blade and rivets of hardened knives silver. Paint one side first, let dry, then paint the other side.

10 mix the blood

Mix piping gel with a few drops of red food coloring. You can keep it translucent or add a sprinkle of cornstarch for a more opaque look. Make a small piping bag from baking parchment (see page 16) and fill with the mixture.

11 prepare piping bag

Twist the top of the filled parchment piping bag to close. Using scissors, snip the end of bag. Take care not to make too big a cut—you want to squeeze out just a dash of "blood," not a gush!

12 apply the blood

Pipe just a trickle of gel onto the icing on each cake at the base of the knife so that it is seeping away from the "wound."

Nothing is more enticing than a disembodied eye—except perhaps a disembodied eye marinating in a thick, glistening pool of sticky goo. Be sure to make a good-size batch of these tantalizing cakes, because everyone will surely want one of their own.

eyeball mini cakes

stuff you'll need

- serrated and craft knives
- 6 x 6 in. (15 cm) square cake boards, about ½ in. (1 cm) thick, covered with white self-adhesive shelf paper
- large piping bag and quick-ice tip
- small curved spatula
- small rolling pin
- modeling tool
- 2½ in. (6 cm) round cutter
- no.1M and no.10 icing tips
- small palette
- paintbrushes
- airbrush
- microwave cooker

food stuff you'll need

- 1 recipe cake batter of choice (see page 11), baked in 12-hole miniball pan
- 4½ cups (1 liter) decorator's buttercream icing (see page 10)
- 1½ lb. (675 g) white fondant
- gel colors: eye color of choice, black, and red
- vodka or lemon extract
- red airbrush color
- 1 cup (235 ml) clear piping gel
- 4 oz. (110 g) red fondant

STUFF YOU'LL NEED TO KNOW

◄ ICING A CAKE
see page 12

◄ ROLLING OUT FONDANT
see page 13

◄ COVERING A CAKE
WITH FONDANT
see page 13

◄ APPLYING PAINT AND
PEARL DUST
see page 16

◄ AIRBRUSHING
see page 17

1 fix cakes to bases

Using a serrated knife, level the flat surfaces of the miniball cake halves. Fix a cake half to each cake board, leveled side up, using a dab of buttercream icing.

2 build the eyeball

Spread a layer of buttercream over the leveled surface of each half-cake on the cake boards, then place another half-cake on top.

3 ice the cakes

Using the large piping bag and quick-ice tip, pipe buttercream icing in an even layer over entire surface of each cake. Smooth the surface of the icing with the curved spatula.

7 paint the eye

Mix gel colors in small palette with a few drops of vodka or lemon extract. Using a small paintbrush, paint iris area of each cake, concentrating darker color around the rim and gradually lighter color toward the pupil. Paint pupil area black.

8 cut out highlight

Roll out a small piece of white fondant, and cut out a round highlight for each cake using small end of no.10 icing tip. Carefully fix fondant highlight to the edge of the pupil area on each cake.

9 paint on the veins

Using a very thin paintbrush and red gel color, paint veins around lower half of each cake in branch-like patterns.

4 cover with fondant

Divide white fondant into six pieces. Roll out each piece into a rough circle—diameter should be width plus height of cake ball times two, plus extra for leeway. Drape fondant over each cake, smoothing on with your hands. Trim off and keep excess.

5 mold and smooth balls

Using modeling tool, tuck in fondant around the base of the cakes to ensure a rounded shape. Smooth surface again with your hands.

6 mark the iris and pupil

Using 2½ in. (6 cm) round cutter, lightly mark the area that will be the iris on each cake, then using the large end of 1M icing tip, mark out pupil.

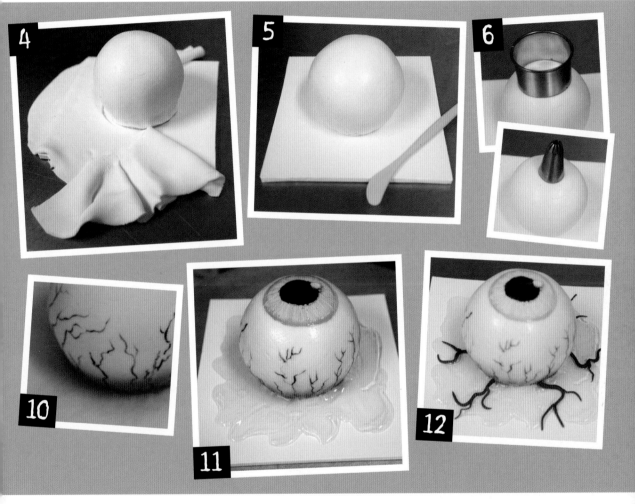

10 add blood

To add depth to the base of the eye, airbrush with a very light coat of red color, concentrating only on the bottom of the eyeball.

11 apply vitreous fluid

Heat clear piping gel in a microwave cooker for a few seconds until slightly runny. Apply gel around the base of each cake using small spatula.

12 add the tendons

Roll out thin snakes of red fondant. Fix around base of each cake, arranging so that they branch out from the cake.

Legend has it that Vincent van Gogh severed his earlobe after a row with fellow artist Paul Gauguin, wrapped it in cloth, and presented it to a prostitute. It has since emerged that more likely the ear was lopped off during a sword fight with Gauguin. Personally, I prefer the proffering of the lobe to the young lady. Has someone ever vowed to give you something of themselves, only to fall short? To avoid all ambiguity, give someone a piece of yourself, preferably in a nice box.

ears to you, dear

stuff you'll need

- rolling pin
- baking parchment
- box, bow, and ear templates
- craft knife
- paintbrushes
- serrated knife
- large piping bag and quick-ice tip
- 12 in. (30 cm) square cake board, about ½ in. (1 cm) thick, covered with white self-adhesive shelf paper
- small spatula
- palette, for mixing color
- ball tool
- airbrush
- scissors

food stuff you'll need

- 1 lb. (450 g) red fondant
- 2 tsp. CMC powder
- 1 recipe vanilla cake batter (see page 11), baked in ¼ sheet pan
- 3 cups (700 ml) decorator's buttercream icing (see page 10)
- 6 oz. (175 g) ivory fondant
- super pearl luster dust
- 1 oz. (25 g) white fondant,
- gold luster dust
- vodka or lemon extract
- red edible marker
- 3 oz. (85 g) modeling chocolate (see page 10)
- fleshtone airbrush color, or fleshtone-colored dust
- 2 tbsp. red piping gel

1 cut out box lid

Mix three-quarters of red fondant with CMC powder and roll out on dusted surface. Cut out piece of baking parchment using heart-shaped box-lid template. Place parchment heart on rolled-out fondant and cut around it with craft knife.

2 cut out lid sides

Use lid-side template to cut out strip of baking parchment. Following outline of parchment strip, cut out two pieces of red fondant with craft knife.

3 attach sides to lid

Using water, applied with a stiff paintbrush, fix the fondant side strips in place around the fondant lid top.

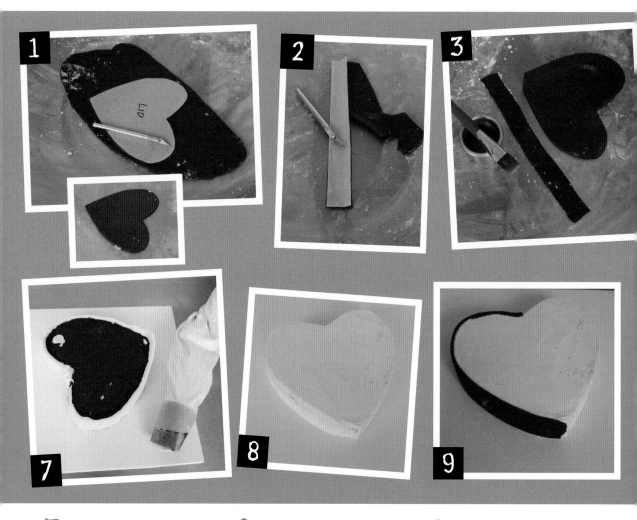

7 attach cake to board

Fill large piping bag fitted with quick-ice tip with the buttercream icing and use to place a dab of icing on each corner of the cake. Turn cake over and place in position on the covered cake board.

8 ice the cake

Pipe more buttercream icing all over the top and sides of cake. Smooth over the entire surface of icing with a small spatula.

9 cut out box sides

Roll out the remaining red fondant. Cut out a strip of baking parchment using the wider template for the box sides. Following the outline of the parchment strip, cut out two strips of red fondant.

4 harden the lid

Leave the assembled box lid in a cool place for at least 24 hours to dry out completely and firm up.

5 fix template on cake

Cut out another piece of baking parchment using the cake heart template. Place on the chilled cake using a dab of buttercream icing to hold in position.

6 cut out cake

Following the outline of the parchment template, carefully cut out the cake heart with the serrated knife.

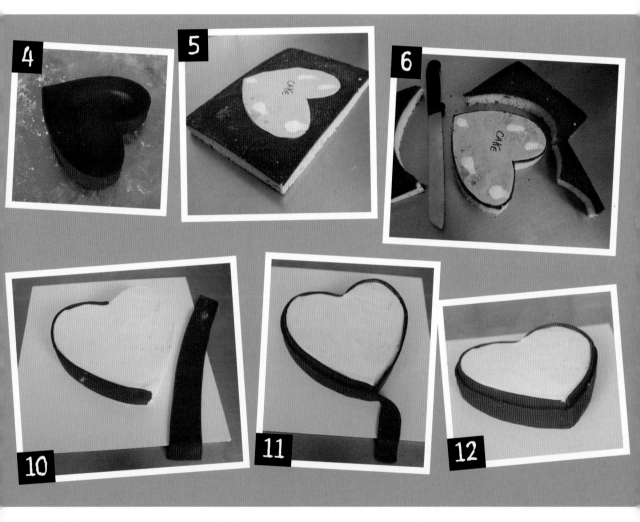

10 attach box sides

Carefully press the red fondant side strips onto the sides of the iced cake. Trim as necessary.

11 cut out narrow strips

Use the narrower box-side template to cut out another baking parchment strip. Follow outline of parchment to cut out two more pieces of red fondant. Fix one piece around lower edge of one side of box, using dabs of water. Trim to fit.

12 fix and trim second strip

Again using dabs of water, fix the second narrow strip of red fondant around lower edge of the other side of the box. Trim as necessary.

13 add lining

Cut out a piece of baking parchment using the box-lining template. Roll out ivory fondant and cut out two oblong pieces, following the outline of piece of parchment. Drape ivory fondant pieces over top of cake in box.

14 fold fondant "fabric"

Arrange the pieces of ivory fondant into soft folds so that they look like crumpled cloth.

15 add pearl dust

Using a fluffy paintbrush, dust the ivory fondant with a light coating of super pearl luster dust so that it resembles satin.

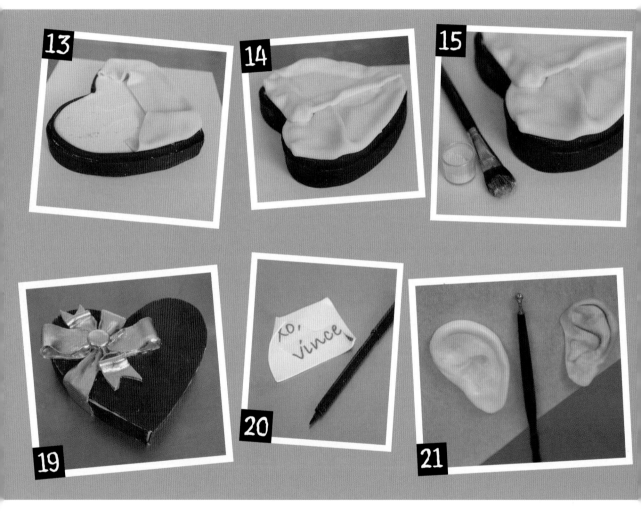

19 allow to dry

Set the box lid with painted bow aside in a cool place for several hours until completely dry.

20 make gift tag

Roll out and cut a small square from leftover white fondant trimmings. Inscribe your message on fondant square using the red edible marker. Curl up corners of note and leave to dry and harden.

21 shape the ear

Roll out the modeling chocolate and cut out a rough ear shape from it using the template. Use ball tool to add fold and crease detailing to ear.

16 cut out bow strips

Using the bow templates, cut out the strip shapes and center disc detail from baking parchment. Roll out white fondant. Following outline of parchment pieces, cut out bow pieces from rolled-out fondant. Reserve trimmings.

17 arrange and position bow

Using photograph as a guide, arrange the white fondant strips into a box shape, pinching together at center. Attach bow to hardened box lid with dabs of water. Fix disc detail in center of bow with another dab of water.

18 paint the bow

Mix gold luster dust with a few drop of vodka or lemon extract to make a thick paint. Using a small paintbrush, carefully paint the bow gold.

22 color the ear

Lightly airbrush or dust fleshtone coloring over the entire surface of the ear. Set aside to dry.

23 place ear in box

Place finished ear on top of folded "fabric" inside the cake box. Arrange the prepared gift tag at the side of the box and fix in place with dab of icing.

24 add blood and cover

Make small piping bag from baking parchment (see page 16) and fill with red piping gel. Cut tip of bag with scissors. Squeeze red gel "blood" onto side of ear in box. Place lid partly over the box, as shown in photograph.

In the 1986 film *Blue Velvet*, a young man comes across a human ear in a field. He begins an investigation to find the owner, resulting in a journey into his hometown's seedy underbelly. This theme of discarded flesh fascinated me. Under what circumstances would you abandon a body part? I wanted to portray the limb as not only lost but also forgotten, and maybe languishing among fallen leaves or weeds. Serve this cake, and you and your guests can concoct your own backstory of the errant limb—a zombie attack, perhaps, or a warning message from mobsters?

chop chop!

stuff you'll need

- 12 x 18 in. (30 x 45 cm) wooden cake board, ½ in. (1 cm) thick
- 12 x 18 in. (30 x 45 cm) piece Astroturf
- hot-glue gun
- 6 ft. (1.8 m) green ribbon, to trim board edges
- airbrush
- scissors
- arm template
- foam core, for arm shape
- craft, serrated, and small paring knives
- large piping bag and quick-ice tip
- spatula
- modeling tool
- rolling pin
- scrub brush
- paintbrushes

food stuff you'll need

- airbrush colors: ivory, red, green, and black
- 1 sheet wafer paper
- 1 recipe red velvet cake batter (see page 11), baked in ¼ sheet pan
- 3 cups (700 ml) decorator's buttercream icing (see page 10)
- 8 oz. (225 g) modeling chocolate (see page 10)
- 1¾ lb. (800 g) white fondant, tinted fleshtone color
- 2 oz. (55 g) white fondant
- black petal dust

1 cover cake board
Cover the cake board with the sheet of Astroturf, using the hot-glue gun to attach turf to board. Fix green ribbon around sides of board with hot-glue gun. Trim excess.

2 make the weeds
Spray ivory airbrush color over one side of sheet of wafer paper. Let dry. Turn sheet over and airbrush other side with ivory color. Let dry, than cut into fine strips of varying lengths to serve as weeds or straw. Set aside.

3 cut out arm shape
Using the arm template as a guide, cut out an arm shape from the foam core using the craft knife.

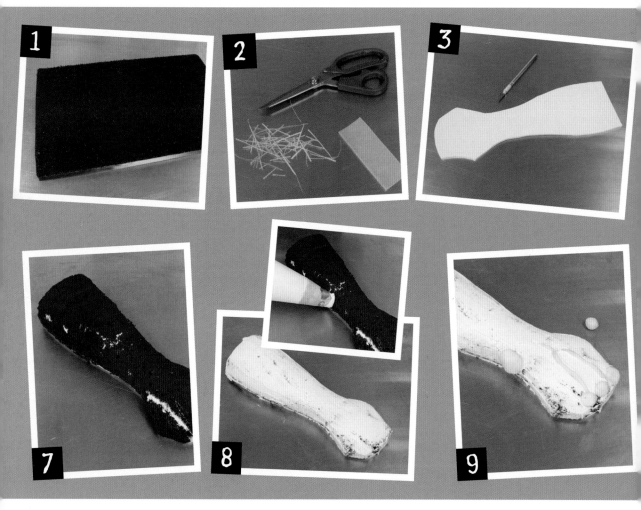

7 carve the cake
Using the small paring knife, carefully carve the top of the arm to create a rounded shape.

8 ice the cake
Pipe buttercream over the top and sides of the arm, using the large piping bag and quick-ice tip. Smooth over the surface of the icing with a spatula.

9 add the details
Roll out balls and snakes of modeling chocolate in varying sizes and use to build up features, such as veins and muscle details, on the arm and hand.

4 cut out cake

Attach the foam arm shape to the top of the chilled cake with a dab of buttercream icing. Following the outline of the arm shape, cut out the cake with the serrated knife.

5 layer with buttercream

Carefully split the cake in half horizontally using the serrated knife. With large piping bag and quick-ice tip, pipe a generous layer of buttercream over cut side of one half. Place other cut half of cake on top.

6 build up arm

Cut out strips of leftover cake and attach with dabs of buttercream to the upper part of the arm to add height and bulk.

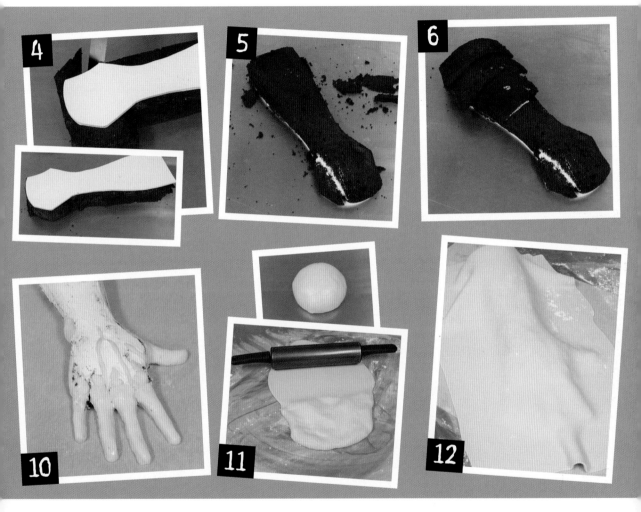

10 make the fingers

Roll out five sausage-shaped pieces of modeling chocolate to form the fingers and the thumb. Attach to hand end of iced cake. Shape and add detail with modeling tool.

11 roll out skin

Roll out the fleshtone-tinted fondant onto a lightly dusted surface to a thickness of about ¼ in. (5 mm).

12 apply the skin

Loosely wrap the rolled-out sheet of fondant around the rolling pin, then carefully unfurl the fondant over the top of the iced cake.

13 trim excess fondant

Carefully trim away excess fondant from around the arm and general hand shape with the craft knife. Tuck cut edges of the fondant neatly under cake. Reserve leftover fondant.

14 shape the fingers

Use craft knife or small paring knife to cut away the fondant around the fingers. With modeling tool, tuck cut fondant edges under the fingers to round them off.

15 flesh out features

With end of modeling tool, carefully press fondant around vein and muscle details to emphasize shape. Mark knuckle detail on fingers and thumb.

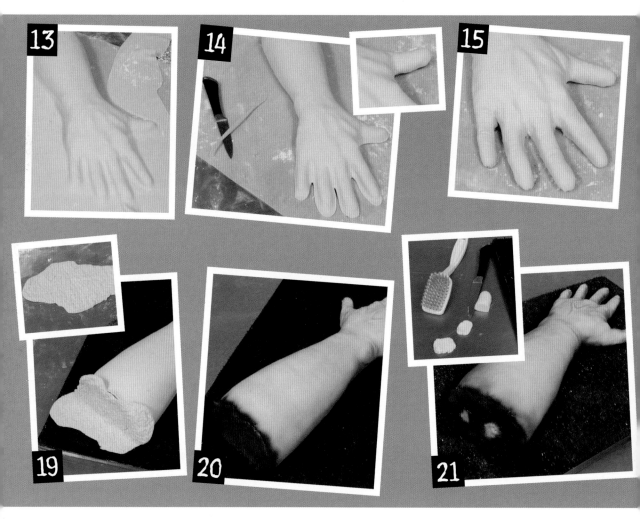

19 make severed end

Roll out a piece of fleshtone-tinted fondant large enough to cover end of the arm. Using scrub brush, indent heavily with texture. Attach to severed end of arm with dabs of water. Trim edges.

20 airbrush on color

Airbrush the severed end of the arm with light coats of red color. Spray light layers of green and black color over the entire arm and hand for a gangrene-ish look.

21 make the bones

Roll out a sausage of white fondant, about ¾ in. (2 cm) thick and 1½ in. (4 cm) long. Cut into two pieces. Fix with water onto severed end of arm. Imprint texture on "bone" ends with scrub brush. Lightly airbrush red.

16 make the nails
Mark out the nails on fingers and thumb with tip of craft knife. Shape nails and add detail with modeling tool.

17 create pores
Press the scrub brush lightly over the entire surface of the fondant skin to create the look of pores. Set cake aside to firm up for 1-2 hours.

18 fix cake to board
Carefully lift cake onto the Astroturf-covered board, using a few dabs of buttercream icing to fix cake in position.

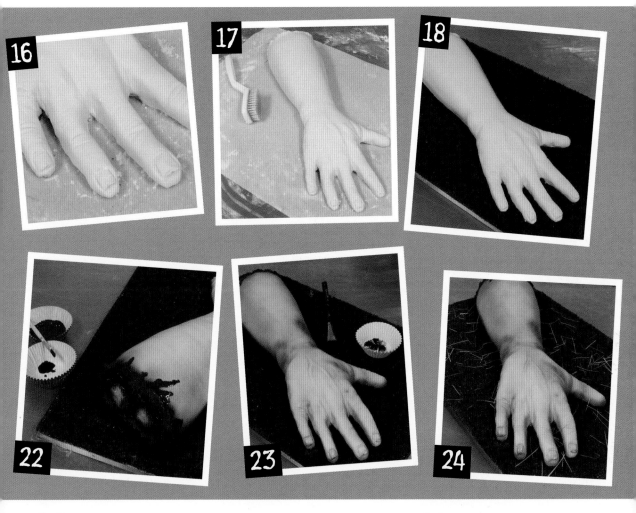

22 add blood
Using a small paintbrush, drip red airbrush color liberally over the severed end of the arm.

23 refine details
Using the modeling tool, pull up the nail ends to create cracked nails. Use black petal dust to emphasize veins and skin creases and to cover arm with a layer of "dirt."

24 scatter the weeds
Scatter the paper weeds, prepared in Step 2, over the Astroturf grass around the arm.

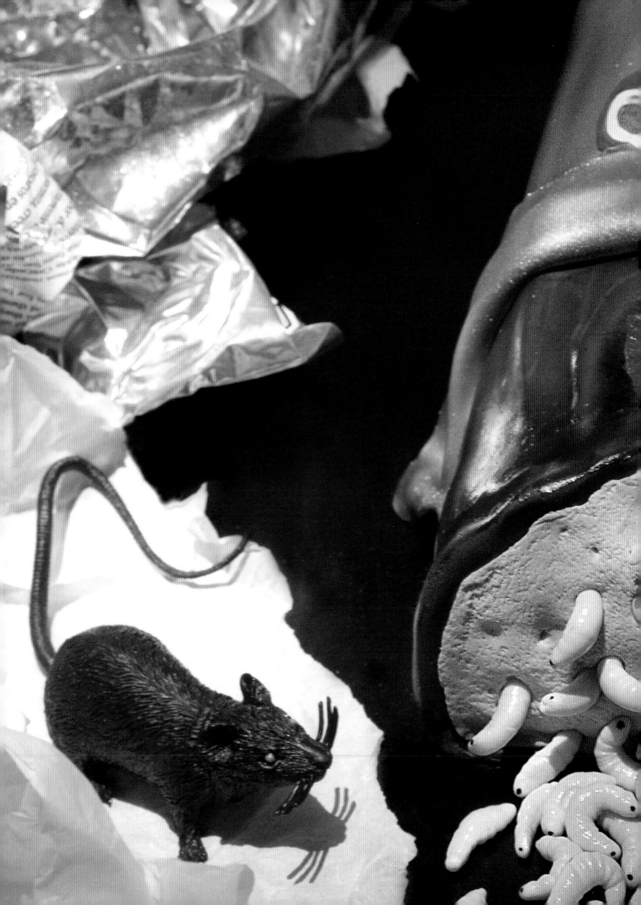

beastly
baking

I have had a lifelong sweet tooth. One day, my sister and I were walking home with the spoils from our day's candy harvest. Eager to satisfy her cravings, she tore into a candy bar. But sensing something was not quite right, she investigated the newly nibbled bar, only to find it was teeming with maggots. The image of that bar with maggots creeping out has stayed with me for decades. Although it did not deter me from eating candy, neither of us ever ate one of those bars again.

lively candy

stuff you'll need

- photocopier
- label and candy bar templates
- baking parchment
- serrated and craft knives
- 10 x 12 in. (25 x 30 cm) wooden cake board, ½ in. (1 cm) thick, covered with black self-adhesive shelf paper
- large piping bag and quick-ice tip
- spatula
- rolling pin
- airbrush
- scrub brush
- light box (optional)
- scissors
- plastic wrap, to protect from airbrush overspray
- modeling tool

food stuff you'll need

- 1 recipe cake batter of choice (see page 11), baked in ¼ sheet pan
- 3 cups (700 ml) decorator's buttercream icing (see page 10)
- 3 oz. (85 g) modeling chocolate (see page 10)
- 1½ lb. (675 g) white fondant
- airbrush colors: chocolate brown, fleshtone, black, and ivory
- 4 oz. (110 g) white fondant, tinted fleshtone color
- 8 oz. (225 g) gray fondant
- silver luster dust
- vodka or lemon extract
- 1 sheet wafer paper
- edible markers
- piping gel
- 3 oz. (85 g) ivory fondant

1 prepare labels and cake

Print out photocopies of label templates. Set aside. Use candy bar template to cut out piece of baking parchment. Attach parchment to chilled cake with dab of buttercream. Following outline, cut candy bar shape from cake with serrated knife.

2 carve candy bar

With serrated knife, carve top edges of the cake until rounded. Slice off one end of cake at an angle to create the "bitten" end. Arrange cake diagonally on the cake board, using dabs of buttercream to hold cake in position.

3 ice the cake

Using large piping bag and quick-ice tip, pipe buttercream icing over the top and sides of cake. Smooth over the icing with a spatula, taking care to maintain the rounded top edges.

7 make nougat filling

Roll out fleshtone-tinted fondant onto dusted surface. Press with scrub brush to create nougat texture. Moisten "bitten" end of bar with water. Fix textured fondant in place. Trim and create more texture with scrub brush. Airbrush "nougat" with fleshtone color.

8 create the wrapper

Roll out gray fondant. Drape over bar, leaving 2 in. (5 cm) exposed at "bitten" end. Trim and tuck in edges. Mix silver luster dust and vodka or lemon extract to milky consistency. Use to airbrush wrapper silver. Add shading with black airbrush color.

9 make the labels

Place sheet of wafer paper over photocopies of labels (made in Step 1). Trace the label outlines and coloring (use light box, if you have one) onto wafer paper with edible markers. Let dry. Carefully cut out labels with sharp scissors.

4 build up "chocolate"

Roll long, thin snakes of modeling chocolate. Apply the snakes along length of iced cake in a curvy pattern to create the swirl detail on the candy-bar coating.

5 cover the cake

Roll out white fondant onto dusted surface. Drape over iced cake. Smooth fondant with hands, tracing around modeling chocolate swirls. Trim excess. Tuck edges of fondant under cake. Pinch around "bitten" end to create sharp edge.

6 color the candy

Avoiding the "bitten" end, spray the candy bar with layers of chocolate brown airbrush color. Spray extra layers of color to create darker shading around swirls to emphasize them.

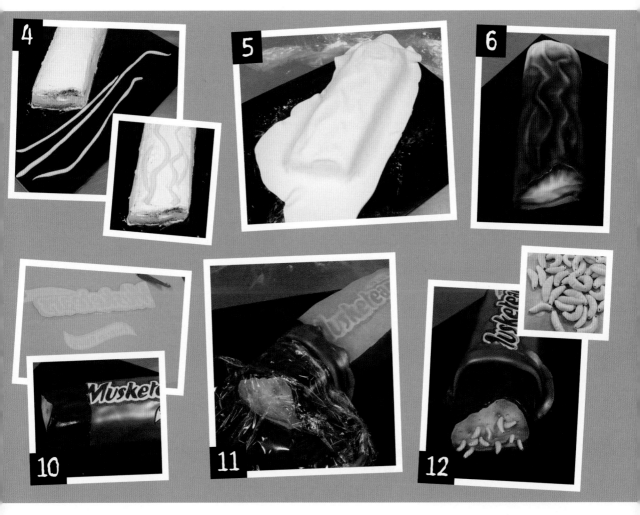

10 attach the labels

Apply a thin coat of piping gel with a spatula onto back of wafer-paper labels. Turn over carefully and place onto candy bar. Lightly smooth to attach.

11 add wrapper edge

Roll out leftover gray fondant. Cut out irregular strip for wrapper edge. Fix to wrapper and fold over. Pinch to shape torn end. Covering exposed candy and labels, airbrush wrapper edge silver. Add shading with strokes of black airbrush color.

12 make the maggots

Roll out snakes of ivory fondant. Cut ¾-1 in. (1-2.5 cm) lengths for maggots. Pinch ends. Roll tip of modeling tool around maggots to mark segments. Curve maggots. Airbrush on ivory color. Let dry. Insert into candy. Scatter maggots around.

The expression to "open a can of worms" means to create new problems inadvertently, often while trying to solve an existing one. However, if your goal is simply to gross out your guests, my can of worms is a piece of cake. It's perfect for the fisherman in your life, the kid who likes shocking their friends, or the gastronome who enjoys sampling new cuisines. This can of worms will have them all fighting over the last morsel.

can of worms

stuff you'll need

- paintbrushes, including a sponge brush
- 12 in. (30 cm) square wooden cake board, ½ in. (1 cm) thick
- rolling pins, large and small
- craft knife
- 14 in. (35 cm) length ⅜ in. (8 mm) doweling
- airbrush
- small bowl
- set of round cutters, including 4.5 in. (11 cm) and 5 in. (13 cm)
- pull tab template
- palette, for mixing paint
- thin cake board
- large piping bag with quick-ice tip
- spatula
- ridged vinyl mat
- modeling tool

food stuff you'll need

- 2 lb. (900 g) white fondant
- airbrush colors: warm brown, ivory, black, and fleshtone
- vodka or lemon extract
- 1 tsp. CMC powder
- silver and gold luster dusts
- 2 x recipe batter of choice (see page 11), baked in ½ sheet pan
- 2 cups (470 ml) decorator's buttercream icing (see page 10)
- chocolate discs, for melting
- 1 cup (110 g) chocolate cookie crumbs
- 6 oz. (175 g) gray fondant
- confectioner's glaze

1 cover the board

Brush cake board surface with water to moisten. Roll out 1 lb. (450 g) white fondant to about ⅛ in. (3 mm) thick. Drape fondant onto moistened board. Smooth over fondant with hands, and trim excess using a craft knife.

2 add wood details

Press 14 in. (35 cm) length of doweling across covered board at 3 in. (7.5 cm) intervals to mark out floor-slat detail in the fondant. Etch wood-grain detail onto fondant surface with craft knife. Apply coat of brown airbrush color over surface with a sponge brush.

3 stain the wood

Soak sponge brush in a bowl of vodka or lemon extract and sweep over painted cake board, removing some color as you go. Repeat until only light wash of color remains; let color that has settled into slats and etching remain. Spray with light coats of ivory airbrush color to even out coloring and emphasize edges.

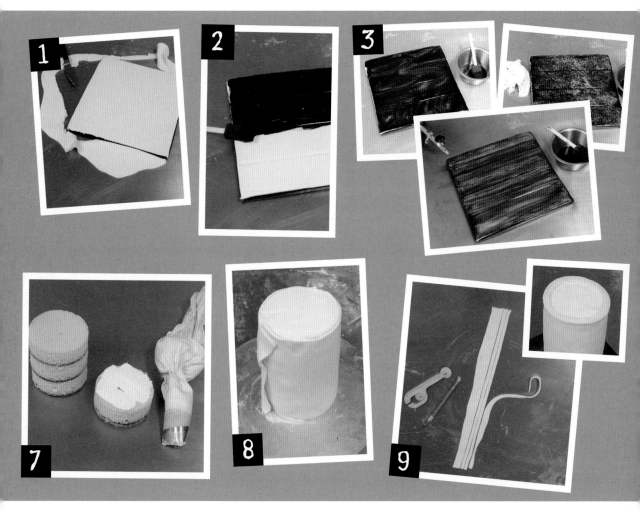

7 stack the cake

Attach cake layer to cake board circle with dab of buttercream. Use large piping bag and quick-ice tip to pipe buttercream onto cake top. Stack second layer. Repeat until all layers are stacked. Pipe icing over cake and smooth with spatula. Chill to firm up.

8 cover the can

Roll out rest of white fondant. Press ridged vinyl mat on fondant to create lined pattern. Trim fondant to approximately circumference and height of iced cake. Roll fondant onto rolling pin and unfurl around chilled cake. Trim excess.

9 create the rims

Roll out fondant trimmings. Cut out circle using 5 in. (13 cm) round cutter, then cut out center of circle with slightly smaller cutter to create cut-top rim detail. Fix to can with water. Cut thin strip for bottom rim detail. Attach with water. Trim.

4 prepare the lid

Combine tsp. of CMC powder with 4 oz. (110 g) white fondant and roll out on dusted surface. Cut out circle for can lid with 4½ in. (11 cm) round cutter. Imprint circular ridge detail on lid using rolled edges of increasingly smaller round cutters. Cut out pull tab using template.

5 finish the lid

Curl up lid edge over length of doweling and leave to dry and set. Mix silver luster dust with vodka or lemon extract to create a thick paint. Repeat with gold luster dust. Paint top of lid and pull tab silver. Paint curled-up, exposed underside of lid gold. Allow pieces to dry.

6 cut out cake

With 5 in. (13 cm) round cutter, cut 4 circles from chilled cake. Use same cutter to mark out circle shapes on thin cake board. Using craft knife, cut circles from cake board.

10 paint the can

Fix cake onto painted board with dabs of buttercream. You may want a supporting dowel on cake board (see page 14) if traveling with cake. Paint can silver, leaving open top unpainted. Airbrush black onto can and prepared lid to add shadows.

11 add lid and soil

Attach pull tab to dried can lid, using a bit of melted chocolate. Hold until set. Fix lid with pull tab in place with a dab of buttercream. Spoon cookie crumbs onto opening and scatter around base of can.

12 make the worms

Roll out ropes of gray fondant to make worms. Pinch and smooth ends. Roll edge of modeling tool around worms to imprint segments. Airbrush with fleshtone color. Brush with confectioner's glaze. While wet, arrange worms in can and on base.

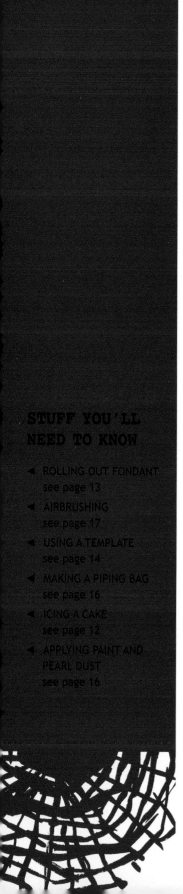

Studies show that the roach is the most reviled creature, besting even rats, spiders, and snakes for the lowest spot. However, the lowly roach can boast an impressive history of survival and is thought to date back 350 million years. I think it's high time the roach got some respect and maybe a little rest and relaxation—at a motel perhaps?

roach motel

stuff you'll need

- 8 x 12 in. (20 x 30 cm) wooden cake board with irregularly cut edges
- rolling pin
- craft knife
- cake pan or similar object, to support board while trimming covering
- craft and serrated knives
- scrub brush
- airbrush
- small cups and palette, for mixing colors
- paintbrushes, including stiff brush
- motel and roach templates
- baking parchment
- scissors
- large icing bag with quick ice tip
- 1 in. (2.5 cm) and 1½ in. (4 cm) square cutters
- small pieces of aluminum foil
- modeling tool
- 6 x 2 in. (5 cm) lengths cloth-covered floral wires, for legs
- 2 x 1½ in. (4 cm) thin silver wires, for antennae

food stuff you'll need

- 1 lb. (450 g) each: white, ivory, and gray fondant
- airbrush colors: black, electric blue, warm brown, green, and dark brown
- white and black gel color
- 2 tsp. CMC powder
- 3 cups (700 ml) decorator's buttercream icing (see page 10)
- 1 recipe cake batter of choice (see page 11), baked in ¼ sheet pan
- silver luster dust
- vodka or lemon extract
- 1 oz. (25 g) each: brown and black fondant
- confectioner's glaze

1 cover the board

Moisten cake board, including edges, with water. Roll out white fondant to about ⅛ in. (3 mm) thick and drape onto board, taking care to cover edges. Smooth over with hands and set board on a cake pan to raise up from table. Trim excess fondant with craft knife around board base. Keep leftover fondant.

2 make the concrete

Press scrub brush into surface of covered board, including edges. Airbrush a light coat of black onto surface, gradually darkening at edges. Place a small amount of white gel and black gel into cups. Dip a stiff paintbrush into white gel. Flick end of brush to spatter color onto board. Repeat with black color.

3 make the sign

Mix half of CMC powder into white fondant trimmings and roll out. Place motel-sign template on fondant and cut out sign shape. Keep trimmings. With template still on fondant, use tip of craft knife to trace a dotted outline of lettering and border onto the fondant strip.

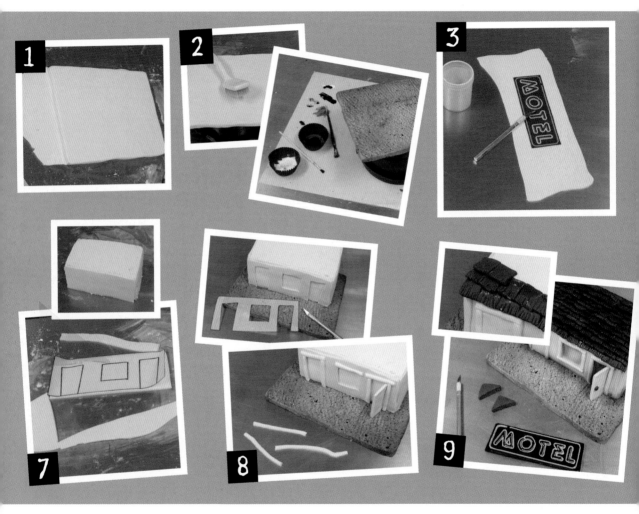

7 cut and fit the walls

Fix cake on board with dab of buttercream. Use piping bag and quick-ice tip to pipe buttercream over cake. Use motel-wall templates to cut out parchment shapes. Roll out ivory fondant. Cut out wall panels, following parchment shapes. Keep trimmings. Press panels onto cake.

8 cut out windows and doors

Hold front-wall template on cake and cut window and doors areas from fondant wall. Roll out white fondant and CMC mix trimmings. Cut out window and doors. Fix in cut-out areas. Cut piece for open door. Use water to attach. Roll out and attach thin strips for door and window frames.

9 add roof and sign

Attach gray fondant door handles with water. Roll out rest of fondant. Cut 1 in. (2.5 cm) squares with cutter. Use craft knife to mark with notches for shingle effect. Fix to roof in overlapping rows. Cut 1½ in. (4 cm) square and cut diagonally to make sign supports. Attach to roof and fix sign on top with water.

4 paint the sign

Flip over the fondant motel sign onto a clean surface. Airbrush sides and back with black color. When dry, turn over and airbrush front (marked) side. Set aside to dry.

5 pipe on neon

Mix a few drops of electric blue airbrush color into 4 oz. (110 g) buttercream until well blended. Make small baking-parchment piping bag (see page 16) and fill with mixture. Snip end. Pipe blue icing over traced outline of the lettering and border. Let dry.

6 cut out cake

Use motel-base template to cut out baking parchment shape. Fix parchment on chilled cake with dab of buttercream and follow outline to cut out three pieces of cake. Stack and sandwich together with buttercream. Holding motel side-wall template on sides of cake, cut angle for roof slant.

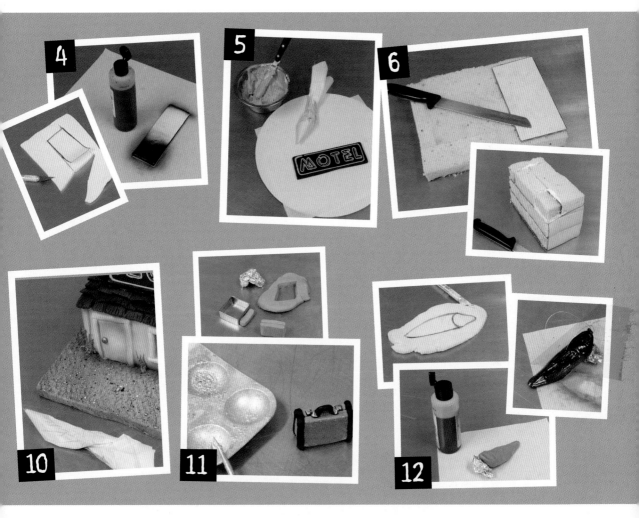

10 add the details

Airbrush black in and around window, doors, and motel base. Make parchment piping bag and fill with buttercream, mixed with warm brown and green color. Snip end. Pipe "weeds" around motel. Mix silver luster dust and vodka or lemon extract and paint doorknobs.

11 make the suitcase

Roll out brown fondant about ½ in. (1 cm) thick. Cut 1½ in. (4 cm) by 1 in. (2.5 cm) piece. Press with crumpled foil to texture. Imprint lid with modeling tool. Roll out black fondant. Cut out latches and case trim. Attach with water. Cut handle. Fix with water. Paint latches silver.

12 make roach and assemble

Mix rest of CMC powder and ivory fondant. Roll out. Use template to cut out roach. Attach fondant balls for eyes. Add detail with modeling tool. Press roach on foil ball to arch up. Fit leg and antennae wires. Airbrush dark brown. Paint on confectioner's glaze. Let dry. Set roach and case in place.

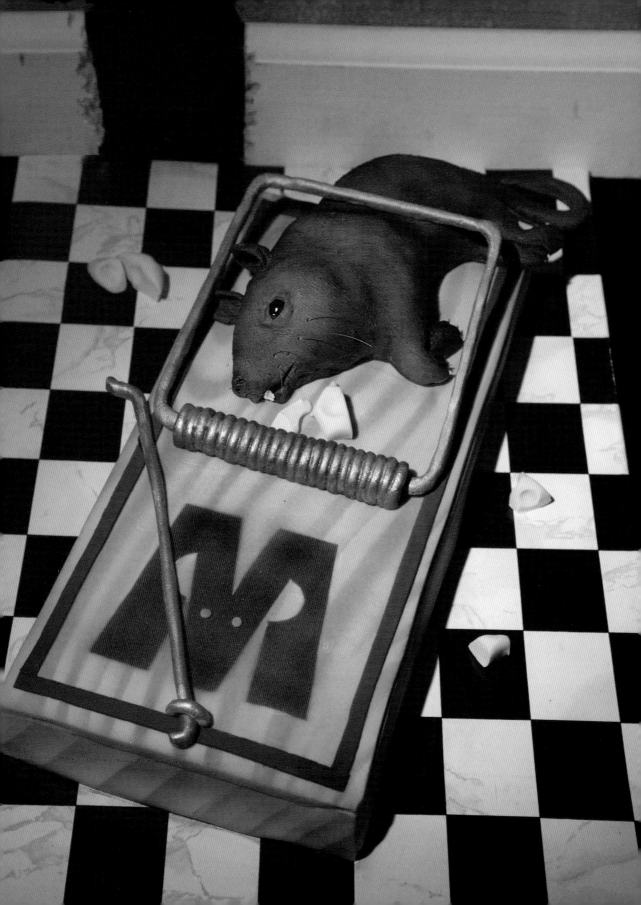

The modern mouse seems to have evolved into an exceptionally elusive and cunning creature. Having had experience trying to trap a rogue mouse, I'm convinced that the mouse's main mission in life is stirring up rage and frustration. Find catharsis by building your own mousetrap in cake and crafting your own mouse "prize." The best part is that no animals need to be harmed in the making of this confection.

mortified mouse

stuff you'll need

- photocopier
- logo and trap-base templates
- sheets of thin cardboard, to make stencils
- craft and serrated knives
- 12 x 18 in. (30 x 45 cm) wooden cake board, ½ in. (1 cm) thick
- checkerboard-pattern self-adhesive shelf liner
- baking parchment
- paintbrushes and palette, for mixing paint
- large piping bag and quick-ice tip
- large and small spatulas
- rolling pin
- ruler
- fondant smoother
- airbrush
- rotary cutter
- modeling tools, including ball tool
- metal mesh pieces, to add tail texture
- black monofilament fishing line, for whiskers

food stuff you'll need

- 2 lb. (900 g) white fondant
- 1 tsp. CMC powder
- luster dusts: gold, silver, and black
- vodka or lemon extract
- 1 recipe vanilla cake (see page 11), baked in ¼ sheet pan
- 3 cups (700 ml) decorator's buttercream icing (see page 10)
- airbrush colors: warm brown, ivory, red, and black
- 2 oz. (55 g) black fondant
- 3-4 rice-cereal treats
- 4 oz. (110 g) modeling chocolate (see page 10)
- 3 oz. (85 g) gray fondant
- 1 oz. (25 g) golden-yellow fondant

STUFF YOU'LL NEED TO KNOW

- ◄ USING A TEMPLATE
  see page 14

- ◄ APPLYING PAINT AND PEARL DUST
  see page 16

- ◄ ICING A CAKE
  see page 12

- ◄ ROLLING OUT FONDANT
  see page 13

- ◄ COVERING A CAKE WITH FONDANT
  see page 13

- ◄ AIRBRUSHING
  see page 17

- ◄ BUILDING DETAILS
  see page 15

- ◄ MAKING A PIPING BAG
  see page 16

1 make logo stencil

Print out a photocopy of the logo template. Glue onto a sheet of thin cardboard. Using a craft knife, cut out around the outline of the logo to make a stencil. Do not cut around the two dots.

2 prepare the board

Cover the top and sides of the wooden cake board with checkerboard-pattern self-adhesive shelf liner so it resembles a tiled floor.

3 prepare the trap

Make trap "hardware" 1-2 days in advance. Cut out a baking parchment shape, using trap-base template. Mix 4 oz. (110 g) white fondant with CMC powder. Roll piece of fondant mixture into a sausage shape, about ¼ in. (5 mm) thick, to form the base of the trap's spring. Set aside.

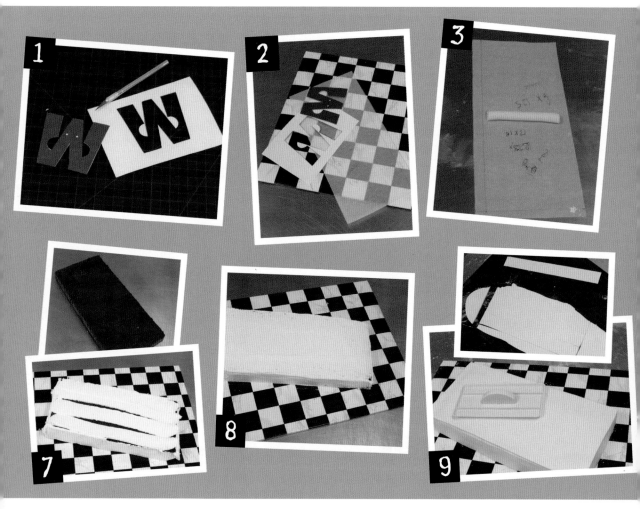

7 prepare the cake

Fix trap-base parchment shape to top of chilled cake with a dab of buttercream and follow outline to cut out cake. Fix cake in place on checkered board with buttercream. Use piping bag and quick-ice tip to pipe buttercream over the cake.

8 smooth the icing

Using the large spatula, carefully smooth the buttercream icing on the top of the cake. Use the small spatula to smooth the icing on the sides, taking care to maintain cake's squared-off edges.

9 cover with fondant

Roll out remaining white fondant onto a dusted surface. Measure sides and top of iced cake and use craft knife and ruler to cut out fondant panels to cover them. Attach to cake. Trim as necessary. Smooth with fondant smoother.

4 make the coils

Roll more of the fondant-CMC mixture into a long, thin snake, about ⅛ in. (3 mm) thick. Cut into pieces, each long enough to wrap around the circumference of the prepared spring base, forming the coils. Place coils close together, attaching with dabs of water.

5 create trap mechanisms

Roll another long, thin snake of fondant-CMC mixture. Use to form three sides of a rectangular shape, as wide as the length of the prepared coiled spring. Roll another long snake of fondant and use to form trap lever, bending ends into shape. Let harden.

6 paint the hardware

Mix gold and silver luster dusts with vodka or lemon extract to make a thick paint. Paint all the prepared trap hardware. Let dry, then lightly brush black luster dust into crevices to create an aged look. Leave the painted hardware in a cool place or refrigerator, for 24 hours to harden.

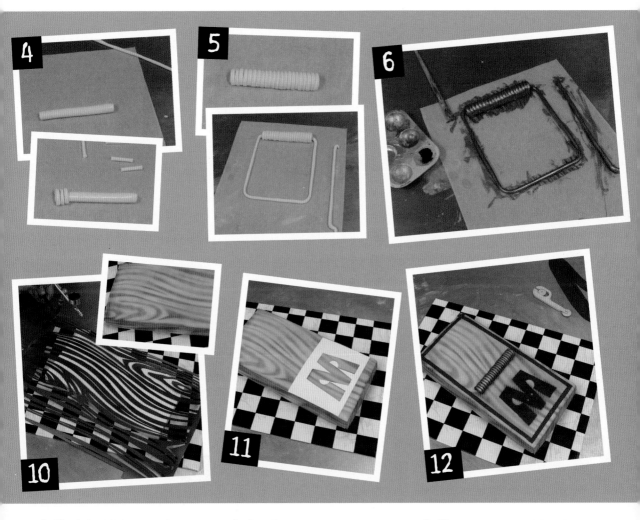

10 airbrush on woodgrain

Use craft knife to cut swirling lines in sheet of cardboard to make a woodgrain stencil. Place stencil on cake and airbrush with warm brown color, creating pattern on top of cake. Repeat on sides. Lightly spray ivory over entire cake. Let dry.

11 airbrush the logo

Place prepared logo stencil in position on cake top. Spray red airbrush color directly onto stencil, avoiding overspray. Remove stencil. Roll out two tiny balls of fondant for the dots. Fix in place on logo with water. Lightly airbrush ivory on logo.

12 start to assemble trap

Roll out black fondant onto dusted surface. Use a rotary cutter to cut out strips about ¼ in. (5 mm) wide, to use as a border trim with cake top. Attach with water. Trim as necessary. Fix prepared coiled spring in place with a dab of water.

13 form the mouse

Squeeze rice-cereal treats tightly together and form into a very rough mouse shape. Squeeze one end into a rounded-off point to form the snout area. Imprint eye socket area with the ball tool.

14 add chocolate features

Press a thin coating of modeling chocolate onto the rice-cereal mouse, building up areas around cheeks and belly. Add a tapering snake of chocolate for the tail and short sausage-like lengths of chocolate for the paws.

15 cover with fondant

Roll out gray fondant onto a dusted surface. Roll fondant around rolling pin and carefully unfurl over the chocolate-covered mouse.

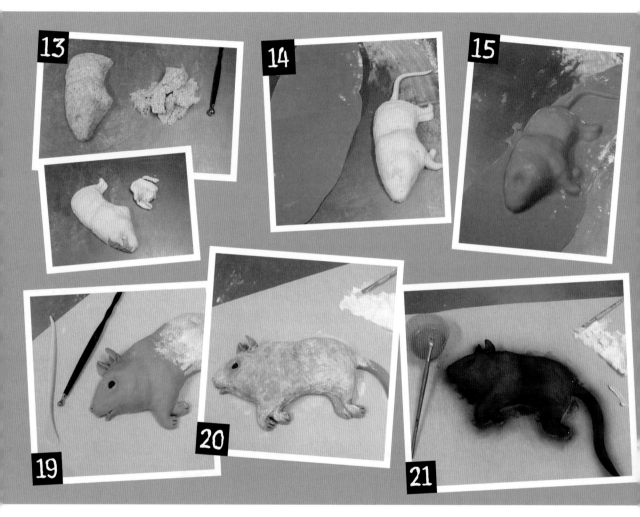

19 add facial features

Roll a small ball of leftover black fondant to form an eye. Lightly moisten indented eye socket area and press eye into it. Use modeling tool to add eye, cheek, mouth, and nostril details.

20 add hair

With a stiff paintbrush, paint buttercream-icing hair over the mouse's entire body and head. Try to mimic the direction of hair growth.

21 color the mouse

Airbrush mouse with light coats of black color. Spray extra color around features to add shading and emphasize details. Make a small baking parchment piping bag (see page 16). Fill with buttercream and use to pipe tiny teeth onto mouse.

16 trim excess fondant
Using a craft knife, carefully cut away the excess fondant. Tuck edges under mouse body and around the tail. Keep fondant trimmings.

17 add detail
Roll out small balls of gray fondant and flatten to form the ears. Pinch ends together and attach to back of mouse head area with a dab of water. Use modeling tool to add detail to the paws.

18 texture the tail
Pressing lightly down with pieces of metal mesh, imprint texture onto the top and sides of the tail.

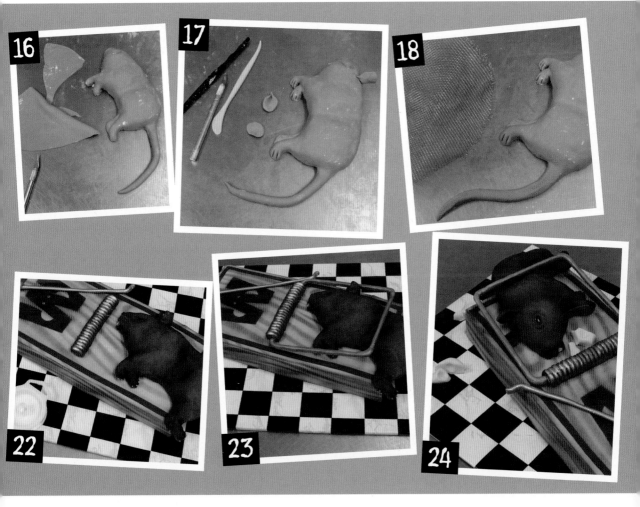

22 set mouse on trap
Carefully position mouse on cake top, fixing in place with a dab of buttercream. Allow back end of mouse and tail to drape onto the checkered "floor." Cut short lengths of black monofilament fishing line for whiskers. Insert into snout area.

23 set the trap
Very carefully place the prepared trap mechanism onto mouse. This piece will be very fragile. If you experience any breakage, you can use a painted, cloth-covered floral wire instead.

24 add the cheese
Cut irregular chunks of golden-yellow fondant and imprint holes on them using a ball tool to form the cheese. Set cheese in place on trap, and scatter a few pieces around the checkerboard floor.

Some insect collections rely on enticing the unsuspecting creatures into jars of formaldehyde—known as killing jars! But butterflies can damage their fragile wings trying to escape, so are suffocated by crushing the thorax. Such is the cruel price of natural beauty.

butterfly collector

stuff you'll need

- tracing paper and pencil
- butterfly and frame templates
- airbrush
- paintbrushes and palette, for mixing paint
- scissors
- sheet of stiff paper
- small Styrofoam block
- 12 in. (30 cm) square wooden cake board, ½ in. (1 cm) thick, covered with black self-adhesive shelf paper
- large piping bag with quick-ice tip
- spatula
- rolling pin
- ridged vinyl mat
- ruler
- craft knife
- 2 black decorator's flower stamens, for antennae

food stuff you'll need

- 2 sheets edible wafer paper
- black edible marker
- sky blue airbrush color
- piping gel
- peacock blue and silver luster dust
- 1 strand thin spaghetti
- 4 oz. (110 g) black fondant
- vodka or lemon extract
- 1 recipe cake batter of choice (see page 11), baked in 10 in. (25 cm) square pan
- 2 cups (470 ml) decorator's buttercream icing (see page 10)
- 1 lb. (450 g) ivory fondant
- 8 oz. (225 g) gray fondant
- confectioner's glaze

1 copy the template

Make a tracing of the butterfly template, or photocopy it. Color in your tracing, if you wish, or find a photograph of a real butterfly to use as a guide.

2 trace the butterfly

Lay a sheet of wafer paper over butterfly tracing. With a black edible marker, trace butterfly outline onto wafer paper. Using light coats, fill in the black areas around wings with the marker. Leave to dry.

3 paint the butterfly

Airbrush a light coat of sky blue over butterfly drawing on wafer paper. Be careful not to oversaturate the paper as it will weaken it and may cause it to disintegrate. Let dry.

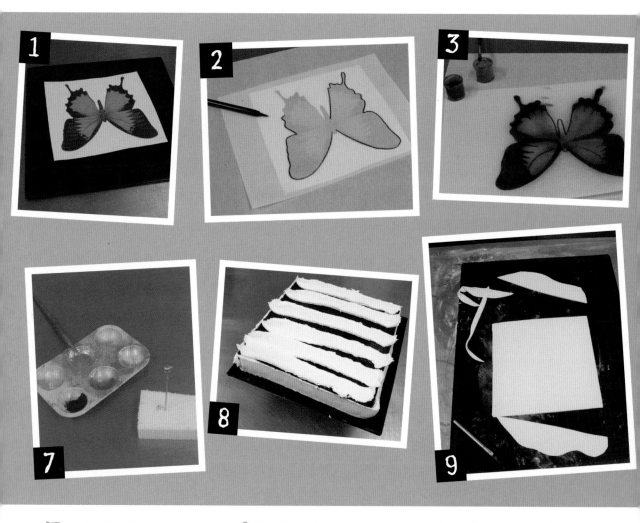

7 make the pin

Break off a 3 in. (7.5 cm) length of spaghetti. Insert into Styrofoam block. Roll small ball of black fondant and fix on top of spaghetti. Mix silver luster dust and vodka or lemon extract into a thick paint. Use to paint spaghetti and fondant ball.

8 ice the cake

Attach chilled cake in position on covered cake board using a dab of buttercream. Pipe buttercream over the top and sides of cake using the large piping bag and quick-ice tip. Smooth icing with a spatula.

9 apply background

Roll out ivory fondant onto dusted surface. Press ridged vinyl mat onto fondant to add texture. Using a ruler and craft knife, cut out a square of fondant large enough to cover top of cake. Apply to iced cake. Trim off any excess.

4 cut out butterfly

When fully dry, flip over butterfly painting onto a clean surface. Brush over a thin coat of piping gel. Fix another sheet of wafer paper to back of butterfly and smooth together. Let dry. Cut out butterfly shape with scissors. Take care with butterfly tails, as they will be fragile.

5 dry and shape wings

Fold a stiff piece of paper down the center to create a raised ridge. Rest the butterfly over ridge to dry, with wings slightly bent down. Leave for 2–3 hours, until gel has set and wings have stiffened.

6 add the luster

With a soft paintbrush, carefully brush dry peacock blue luster dust over the blue portions of the wings to create the powdery sheen that is often seen on the wings of butterflies.

10 make the mount

Roll out black fondant onto dusted surface. Using a ruler and craft knife, cut out four 10 x 2 in. (25 x 5 cm) strips to form the black framing mount around butterfly. Use water to fix around top edges of cake.

11 make the frame

Roll out gray fondant. Use frame template to cut out four mitered pieces. Fix to top edges of cake with water. Cut four 10 x 2 in. (25 x 5 cm) gray fondant strips. Use water to fix to sides of cake. Brush frame with confectioner's glaze.

12 position the butterfly

Fix butterfly on cake with piping gel. Prop up wings with balls of ivory fondant, if needed. Roll out small rope of black fondant, narrowing at one end. Fix on center of butterfly. Insert stamens as antennae. Push prepared pin into butterfly.

twisted
playtimes

Perhaps the oldest graffiti is the art found in the Chauvet Cave in France. Clearly the desire to leave one's mark is an ancient one. Modern graffiti ranges from a simple scrawl to elaborate master-pieces. My own shop has been the target of the lesser graffiti artist, and annoyed with the rudimentary "skills" of these artists, I've often dreamed of lending these miscreants some art criticism. Here's a tastier way to foster the talents of your fave graffiti artist.

baked graffiti

stuff you'll need

- rolling pin
- paintbrushes, including sponge brush
- 14 x 20 in. (35 x 50 cm) wooden cake board, ½ in. (1 cm) thick
- scrub brush
- airbrush
- 2 small cups for paint
- 6 ft. (1.8 m) length black ribbon
- hot-glue gun
- scissors
- 3½ in. (8.5 cm) and 1 in. (2.5 cm) round cutters, and small icing tip
- serrated knives, small paring and craft knives
- thin cake board
- large piping bag with quick-ice tip
- spatula
- ruler
- modeling tools, including ball tool
- toothpick
- spraycan logo templates

food stuff you'll need

- 3 lb. (1.3 kg) white fondant
- airbrush colors: black and white
- 2 x recipe cake batter of choice (see page 11), baked in ½ sheet pan, or 1 recipe vanilla cake batter and 1 recipe devil's food cake batter, each baked in ¼ sheet pan
- 4½ cups (1 liter) decorator's buttercream icing (see page 10)
- silver highlighter
- 1 oz. (25 g) red fondant
- 1 sheet wafer paper
- edible markers
- piping gel

STUFF YOU'LL NEED TO KNOW

◄ ROLLING OUT FONDANT
see page 13

◄ AIRBRUSHING
see page 17

◄ CARVING A CAKE
see page 15

◄ ICING A CAKE
see page 12

◄ COVERING A CAKE
WITH FONDANT
see page 13

◄ APPLYING PAINT AND
PEARL DUST
see page 16

1 prepare the board

Roll out half the white fondant onto a dusted surface. Using sponge brush dipped in water, moisten the surface of the wooden cake board.

2 cover the board

Loosely roll the sheet of white fondant around the rolling pin and carefully unfurl it over the moistened board. Smooth over gently.

3 texture the sidewalk

Press head of scrub brush lightly at random into entire surface of fondant on the board to create rough texture of an urban sidewalk. Do not trim excess fondant until this is complete as it will stretch throughout the imprinting process.

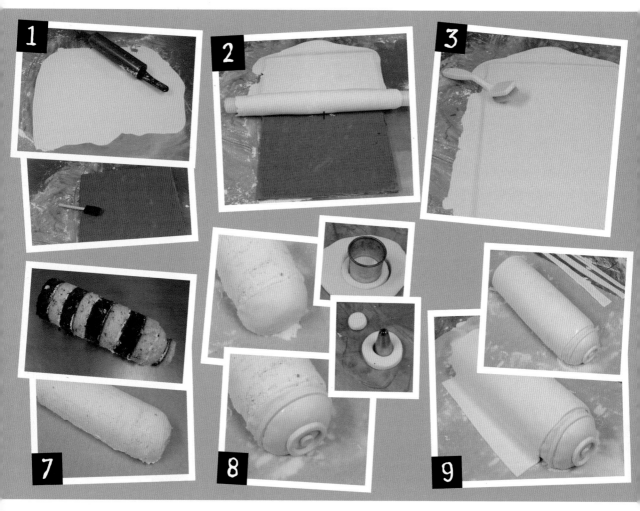

7 assemble cake layers

Cut thin cake board to size of cake layers laid side by side on flat edges. Use buttercream icing to fix layers to cake board and each other. Put rounded-off layer at one end. Pipe over icing with piping bag and quick-ice tip. Smooth with spatula.

8 create nozzle area

Roll out piece of white fondant. Cut circle with 3½ in. (8.5 cm) cutter. Press onto rounded end of cake and trim. Cut strip and attach with water to circle edge. Cut out nozzle detail with 1 in. (2.5 cm) cutter and ends of small icing tip. Attach with water.

9 cover the can

Measure the length and circumference of your "can." Roll out remaining white fondant and cut out rectangle to that size. Drape over iced cake. Trim excess and carefully tuck edges under the cake.

4 color the sidewalk

Airbrush the fondant sidewalk surface very lightly with several coats of black airbrush color, add extra coats of color at edges to emphasize them.

5 complete the sidewalk

Pour white and black airbrush colors into separate small cups. Dip a paintbrush into each color and splatter it onto airbrushed sidewalk, using a flicking motion to create stippled stone effect. Attach black ribbon around edge of board with a hot-glue gun. Trim as necessary.

6 cut out cake

Using 3½ in. (8.5 cm) round cutter, cut out 9 circles of cake. If you wish, you can use a mix of vanilla and devil's food cake. Slice end off each cake circle to create a flat surface. Use small paring knife to round out the top surface of one cake layer.

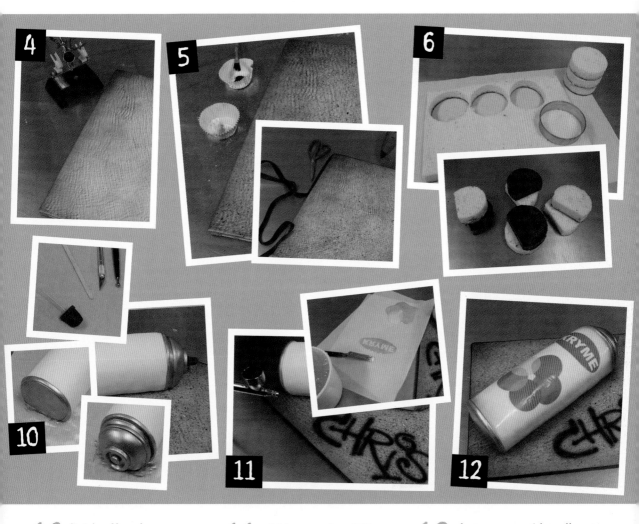

10 finish off ends

Cut 3.5 in. (8.5 cm) fondant circle. Fix to "can" base with water. Cut thin strip for base edge. Fix with water. Paint can top and base with silver highlighter. Use modeling tools to shape nozzle from red fondant Mark hole with edible marker. Mount on toothpick and insert into cake.

11 add logo and graffiti

Trace spraycan logo templates onto wafer paper with edible markers. Cut out labels with sharp scissors. Brush thin coat of piping gel on back of labels and carefully place on cake. Use black color to airbrush graffiti directly onto prepared wooden cake board.

12 place can on sidewalk

Smear buttercream onto the prepared wooden cake board, where you wish to position cake. Carefully lift cake (still on thin cake board) and place on the cake board sidewalk.

The fear of clowns is so pervasive that there is even a special term for it—*coulrophobia*. Studies have shown that children tend to react strongly to the sight of a familiar body that has a strange face. I hear that many adults are similarly creeped out by these overly made-up merrymakers. Here's a clown that doesn't hide behind a jolly countenance. It should prove to be the perfect offering for that annoying tot in your life, or for a phobic friend.

creepy clown

stuff you'll need

- photocopier
- clown head and bow-tie templates
- scissors
- serrated, small paring, and craft knives
- 18 in. (45 cm) round wooden cake board, ½ in. (1 cm) thick, covered with black self-adhesive shelf paper
- large piping bag and quick-ice tip
- spatula
- modeling tool
- rolling pin
- palette, for mixing paint
- paintbrushes
- 2 in. (5 cm) round cutter
- airbrush
- no.2A icing tip

food stuff you'll need

- 1 recipe red velvet cake batter (see page 11), baked in ¼ sheet pan
- 3 cups (700 ml) decorator's buttercream icing (see page 10)
- 6 oz. (175 g) modeling chocolate (see page 10)
- 3 lb. (1.3 kg) white fondant
- gel colors: blue, white, and black
- 8 oz. (225 g) red fondant
- confectioner's glaze
- airbrush colors: ivory and black
- 4 oz. (110 g) purple fondant
- 2 oz. (55 g) yellow fondant
- white cotton candy

1 prepare templates

Print photocopies of the clown head and bow-tie templates. Use a pair of sharp scissors to cut out both of the photocopied paper templates.

2 cut out clown head

Attach the copied clown head template to the top of the cake with a few dabs of buttercream icing. Using the serrated knife and following the outline of the template, cut out the basic head shape of clown.

3 carve out features

With the serrated knife, round off the edges of the cake. Use the small paring knife to hollow out the eye sockets and to shape the cheek and chin areas.

7 paint the eyes

Mix blue and white gel colors together to create two different shades of blue paint. Use to color eye area, painting from light blue in the center to darker blue at edge. Paint on iris with black gel color.

8 add the greasepaint

Apply makeup around eyes and lips with lighter blue paint. Roll out small piece of red fondant. Cut out 2 in. (5 cm) circle with round cutter. Smooth onto nose, fixing with water. Brush confectioner's glaze over nose, mouth, and eye coloring.

9 airbrush details

Lightly airbrush ivory color onto the teeth for a yellowed look. Spray a very light coat of black airbrush color around the features to create shadows and depth.

4 ice the cake

Attach the cake in position on the covered cake board with dabs of buttercream. Using the large piping bag and quick-ice tip, cover the top and sides of cake with buttercream. Smooth over icing with the spatula. Take care to smooth icing into eye sockets and hollowed-out cheek areas.

5 build up details

Using clown head template as reference, build up facial features with pieces of modeling chocolate. Use small sausages of chocolate to create lips and a knitted-brow look. Use balls of chocolate for the chin, cheekbones, and nose. Roll out and flatten larger balls to create ears. Add detail with modeling tool.

6 cover with fondant

Roll out white fondant onto a dusted surface. Wrap loosely around rolling pin and carefully unfurl over iced cake. Smooth over and use tip of modeling tool to trace carefully around features. Trim excess and tuck edges under. Roll small fondant balls for teeth. Pinch into shape. Fix to mouth area with dabs of water.

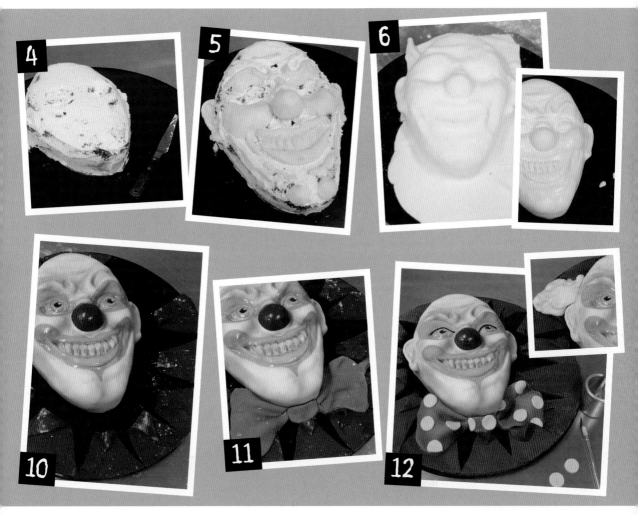

10 create the hoop

Roll out rest of red fondant onto a dusted surface. Use craft knife to cut out 16-18 triangles of varying sizes. Attach around edge of cake board, with bases of triangles overlapping edge of board. Curl back pointed ends.

11 make bow tie

Roll out purple fondant onto a dusted surface. Using the photocopied bow-tie templates, cut out parts from fondant. Arrange bow parts under the clown's chin, attaching with dabs of water. Pinch bow ends to shape and create folds.

12 add final touches

Roll out yellow fondant onto a dusted surface. With small end of 2A icing tip, cut out polka dots. Fix with water onto bow tie. Just before presenting cake, pinch off clumps of cotton candy for hair. Set in place. Avoid getting cotton candy wet.

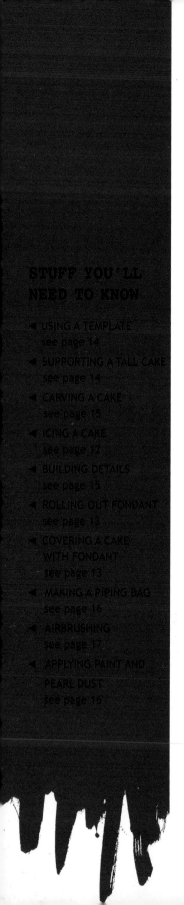

When I was a young, I made sure I meted out equal amounts of attention on all my toys. As time wore on, though, I found myself playing with some toys less and less. What happened to those toys I once so loved? I convinced myself that they had found their way into new homes with new little girls to care for them. But could they have fallen into less loving hands? Observe this cake as a cautionary tale.

terrified teddy

stuff you'll need

- ⅜ in. (8 mm) and ⅛ in. (3 mm) doweling
- drill
- 12 in. (30 cm) square wooden cake board, ½ in. (1 cm) thick
- no.6 wood screw
- teddy bear templates
- baking parchment
- serrated and craft knives
- 4 in. (10 cm) and 5 in. (13 cm) round cutters
- large piping bag and quick-ice tip
- thin cake board
- curved spatula
- rolling pin
- scrub brush and piece of metal mesh, for texturing
- ruler
- modeling tools, including ball tool
- stitching wheel
- 2 toothpicks
- airbrush
- paintbrushes

food stuff you'll need

- 2 x recipe cake batter of choice (see page 11), baked in ¼ sheet pan and 2 halves of 6 in. (15 cm) sports ball pan
- 2 cups (470 ml) decorator's buttercream icing (see page 10)
- 8 oz. (225 g) modeling chocolate (see page 10)
- 2 lb. (900 g) brown fondant
- chocolate discs, melted
- 2 oz. (55 g) each black and white fondant
- dark brown airbrush color
- confectioner's glaze
- silver luster dust
- vodka or lemon extract
- white cotton candy

1 fix dowel to board

Cut 6 in. (15 cm) length of ⅜ in. (8 mm) doweling. Drill pilot hole into corner of cake board. Drill pilot hole into end of doweling and screw into cake board using no.6 screw.

2 cut out cake

Use bear-leg template to cut out two pieces of baking parchment. Attach parchment pieces to chilled cake with dabs of buttercream and follow outline to cut out legs with serrated knife. Use round cutters to cut out a 4 in. (10 cm) and a 5 in. (13 cm) circle of cake.

3 stack the cake

Apply a dab of buttercream to cake board around dowel. Carefully push 5 in. (13 cm) round cake over doweling onto board. Use large piping bag with quick-ice tip to pipe buttercream over top of cake layer, then stack 4 in. (10 cm) round cake on top.

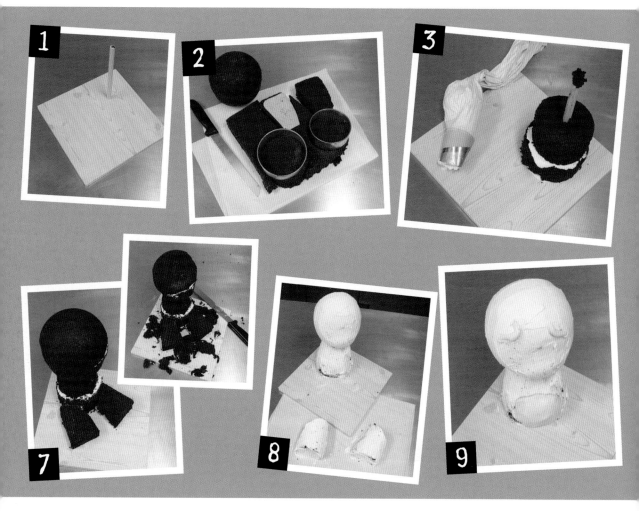

7 attach the head

Attach head on top of cake with a dab of buttercream. Carve into shape, narrowing sides to form jaw and chin. Make a horizontal cut from forehead down to mouth area and round slightly to form muzzle area.

8 ice the cake

Cover the entire cake with buttercream icing using large icing bag and quick-ice tip. Smooth icing with curved spatula. Place leg pieces on a sheet of baking parchment and pipe icing over them. Smooth icing.

9 build the details

Form flattened ball shape from modeling chocolate. Place on body to create fat belly. Roll two 2 in. (5 cm) snakes of chocolate. Curve upward and place on each side of brow area. Curving pieces up slightly gives the teddy a frightened expression.

4 carve body shape

With serrated knife and using angled movements, carve the stacked cake layers until they form a slightly conical shape. To get idea of finished cake, set leg pieces in place.

5 add the supports

Cut three 4 in. (10 cm) lengths of ⅛ in. (3 mm) doweling. Insert into top of cake. Pipe buttercream onto top of cake. Cut out 4 in. (10 cm) circle from thin cake board and cut ⅜ in. (8 mm) hole in center. Slip cake board circle over large dowel and onto iced top of cake.

6 prepare the head

With the piping bag and quick-ice tip, pipe a layer of buttercream over the flat surface of one half-ball of cake. Place the other half-ball of cake on top to form the teddy's head.

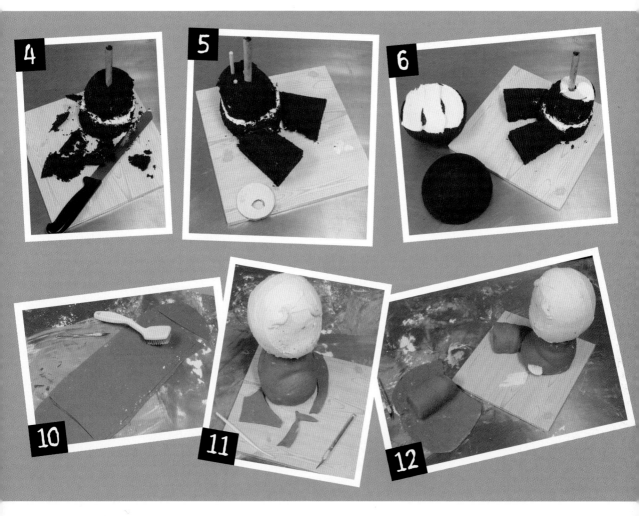

10 roll out fondant

Roll out half of brown fondant onto dusted surface. Press scrub brush randomly into fondant to imprint fur texture. Using ruler and craft knife, cut out a rectangle, measuring approximately the height and circumference of bear's body.

11 cover the body

Wrap fondant piece around body. Smooth onto cake, rounding over chocolate on belly. Trim as necessary. With modeling tool, add definition to body, pressing in folds and creases to give the teddy a slouchy appearance.

12 cover the legs

Roll out more brown fondant and press on scrub brush to give fur texture. Cut in half and drape piece over each leg. Trim to fit. Attach legs to body with dabs of icing. Add creases with modeling tool. Pinch feet to create paw detail.

13 add stitching detail

While fondant on body and legs is still soft, add stitching detail. Roll stitching wheel tool along center of body to create two rows of stitching. Repeat at sides of legs and around feet.

14 prepare head covering

Roll out a large circle of brown fondant. Press with head of scrub brush to imprint with a fur-like texture.

15 cover head

Drape fondant circle over iced head and quickly smooth and stretch simultaneously. Tuck under in chin area. Trim as necessary. Use modeling tool to emphasize facial details. Add stitching detail with stitching wheel around sides and top of head.

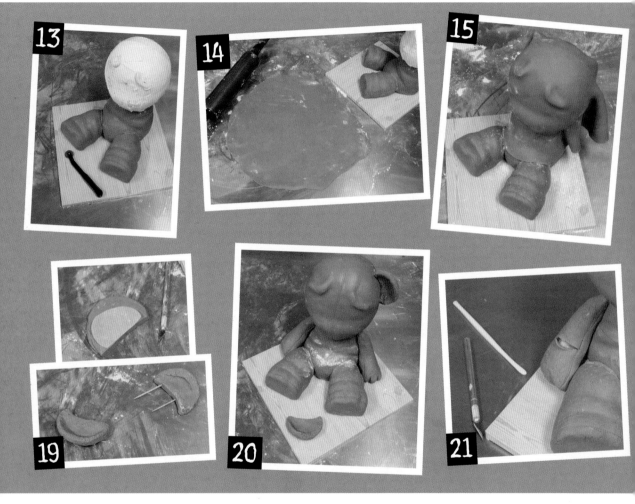

19 make the ears

Use ear template to cut out piece of baking parchment. Follow outline of parchment to cut ear shapes from rolled-out brown fondant trimmings. Add texture with scrub brush. Curve edges to make ear folds. Insert toothpicks into one ear.

20 attach the ears

Pipe a small bead of melted chocolate onto inner edge of ear with toothpicks. Carefully insert ear into side of head. Hold in place until set. Leave second ear on board. With stitching tool, add detail along outer edge of ears.

21 create rips

With a craft knife, make random slits wherever you desire in the fondant covering on the body and head. Pull back the edges of the openings with modeling tool.

16 form the arms

Using the template as a guide and with the serrated knife, carve out the basic arm shapes from pieces of modeling chocolate. Use modeling tool to create the paw area details.

17 cover the arms

Roll out remaining brown fondant on dusted surface. Press with end of scrub brush to imprint with fur texture. Cut out and drape a piece over each chocolate arm. Tuck under and around arms. Trim excess.

18 attach the arms

Make small piping bag from baking parchment (see page 16). Fill with melted chocolate, twist to close and snip end. Apply melted chocolate to underside of one arm. Attach to body. Hold in place until set. Repeat for second arm. Add detail to side of arms with stitching wheel.

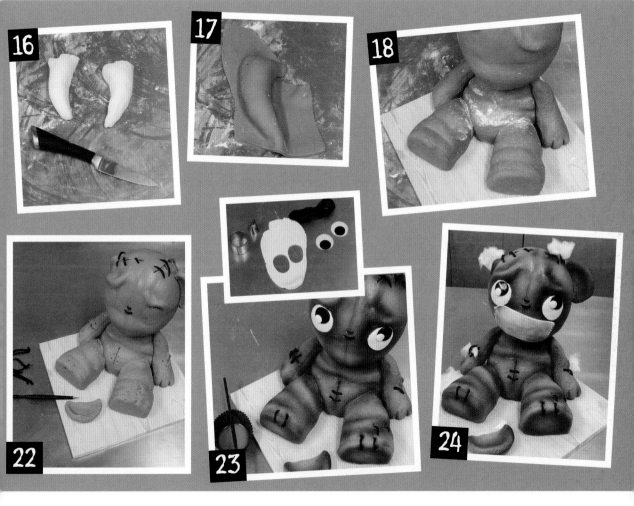

22 make the thread

Roll out black fondant onto dusted surface. Cut out small strips, about ⅛ in. (3 mm) wide. Poke small holes onto either side of "rips," using small ball tool. Insert black fondant thread ends into holes. Trim as necessary.

23 add shading and eyes

Airbrush on dark brown shadows. Roll out white fondant and black fondant trimmings. Cut white circles for eyes. Attach to bear with water. Cut smaller black circles for irises. Fix with water. Cut out white highlights. Attach with water. Brush confectioner's glaze over eyes.

24 finish the bear

Cut out 2 x 5 in. (5 x 13 cm) white fondant strip. Press with metal mesh to texture. Shred ends. Fix on mouth area with water. Curl edges away slightly. Paint with mixture of silver luster dust and vodka or lemon extract. Apply white cotton candy pieces to ripped areas.

for better
for worse

Until the 1960s, marriage was mandatory. Today, we become betrothed by choice, not mandate. Despite staggering divorce rates, marriage is far from an antiquated tradition. Celebrate your nuptials with this tattoo-inspired paean to lasting love.

twisted bridal cake

stuff you'll need

- paintbrushes, including sponge brush
- 10 x 18 in. (25 x 45 cm) wooden cake board, ½ in. (1 cm) thick, covered with black self-adhesive shelf paper
- rolling pin
- craft and serrated knives
- airbrush
- feather, wing, heart, and banner templates
- pencil
- scissors
- rotary tool
- paper towels or plastic wrap, for drying feathers
- large piping bag and quick-ice tip
- curved spatula
- toothpicks
- modeling tools, including ball tool
- 1 in. (2.5 cm) round cutter

food stuff you'll need

- 1 lb. (450 g) black fondant
- airbrush colors: black, white, red, and ivory
- 4-6 sheets wafer paper
- 8 oz. (225 g) white fondant
- piping gel
- 1 tsp. CMC powder
- 1 recipe red velvet cake (see page 11), baked in ¼ sheet pan
- 2 cups (470 ml) decorator's buttercream icing (see page 10)
- 8 oz. (225 g) modeling chocolate (see page 10)
- 1 lb. (450 g) red fondant
- 4 oz. (110 g) ivory fondant
- black edible marker

STUFF YOU'LL NEED TO KNOW

◄ ROLLING OUT FONDANT
see page 13

◄ AIRBRUSHING
see page 17

◄ USING A TEMPLATE
see page 14

◄ CARVING A CAKE
see page 15

◄ ICING A CAKE
see page 12

◄ BUILDING DETAILS
see page 15

1 prepare fondant fabric

Using a sponge brush, lightly moisten surface of covered cake board with water. Roll out the black fondant on a dusted surface to about ⅛ in. (3 mm) thick. Cut fondant into three or four pieces.

2 cover the board

Drape a piece of black fondant onto the board, arranging in soft folds to resemble fabric. Repeat, overlaying the pieces until board is fully covered. Trim excess from sides with craft knife. Reserve leftover fondant.

3 airbrush the fabric

To achieve a satin-like look, airbrush the fondant with black and white airbrush colors. Spray light coats of black in the recessed areas. Spray highlights of white onto the raised areas of "fabric."

7 create wing supports

Mix remaining white fondant with CMC powder. Roll out and use template to cut out two wing shapes. Guided by template, roll two snakes of fondant to form top part of wings. Fix fondant snakes to wing shapes with water.

8 start to assemble wings

Starting from the bottom, attach a row of large feathers to a wing support using beads of piping gel. Attach a second row of large feathers, slightly overlapping the row below.

9 finish the wings

Continue attaching overlapping rows of feathers to wing support until it is densely covered, moving on from large to small feathers. Cover second wing with feathers in same way. Set wings aside to dry on paper towels or plastic wrap.

4 cut out feathers

Using feather templates, trace 40-50 large feathers and 30-40 small feathers onto wafer paper with a pencil. Cut out feathers, using sharp scissors. Cut notches, angled toward center, along edges of feathers.

5 make the ribs

Roll out white fondant onto a dusted surface. Using rotary cutter, cut out thin strips of fondant, about ⅛ in. (3 mm) wide, one for each feather.

6 finish the feathers

Brush piping gel down center of feathers. Apply to just a few feathers at a time. Place a white fondant strip into center of feathers to create the rib. Trim as necessary. Repeat with rest of feathers. Set aside to dry.

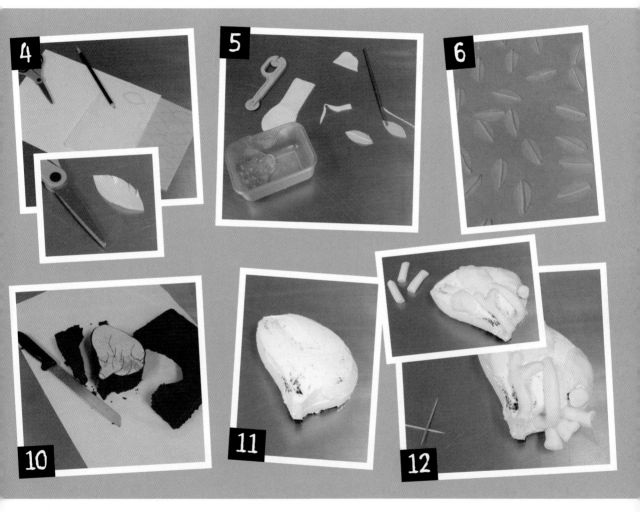

10 carve the cake

Attach heart template to chilled cake with a dab of buttercream. Carve out basic shape with serrated knife. Remove template. Slightly round edges with serrated knife. Carve ventricle shapes and round slightly.

11 ice the cake

Using large piping bag and quick-ice tip, cover cake with buttercream icing. Smooth the surface of icing with a curved spatula, taking great care to maintain shape of the rounded carved areas.

12 build up details

Roll out small snakes of modeling chocolate and, using template as a guide, attach to heart surface to provide details of ventricles and atria. If needed, insert toothpicks into chocolate pieces to attach them to heart.

13 cover the heart

Roll out red fondant onto a dusted surface to about ¼ in. (5 mm) thick. Roll fondant loosely around rolling pin and carefully drape over the prepared cake heart.

14 smooth on fondant

Smooth fondant over the surface of iced heart, carefully pushing it in and around the details. Trim excess and tuck edges under.

15 detail the heart

Using modeling tools, add details to the heart. Trace around parts to emphasize them. Insert ball tool into atria and press gently to create the hollow areas.

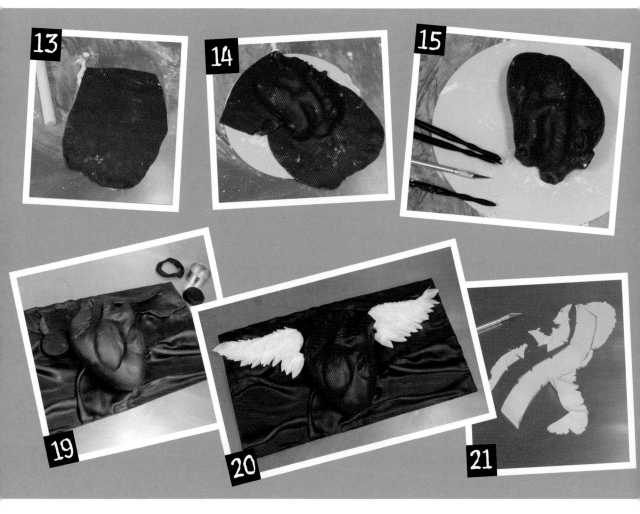

19 add wing supports

Roll out leftover black fondant onto dusted surface. Using 1 in. (2.5 cm) round cutter, cut out two black fondant circles. Place a circle on either side of the heart on the board. These will serve as supports, or risers, for the wings.

20 attach the wings

Apply a small amount of piping gel or buttercream to wing supports as glue for the wings. Gently set the wings in place. Handle the wings with great care as the feathers will be very fragile.

21 cut out banner

Roll out ivory fondant onto a dusted surface. Using template, cut out banner shape with the craft knife.

16 airbrush the heart

Spray several light coats of red airbrush color over entire surface of the heart to deepen the color.

17 add shadows

Using black airbrush color, lightly spray shadows around the bottom and parts of heart to emphasize them. Set aside to dry.

18 set heart on board

Place the prepared heart onto the center of covered cake board. Use a few dabs of buttercream icing to fix in place.

22 inscribe the banner

Guided by the lettering on the banner template, draw the word *forever* on fondant banner with black edible marker. Make sketchy outlines along the top and bottom edges of the banner for a vintage tattoo effect.

23 age the banner

Lightly spray the edges of the banner with ivory airbrush color to give it a look of aged parchment.

24 arrange the banner

Set banner in place, attaching to heart with a dab or two of buttercream or piping gel. Gently curl ends over sides of heart. Using tip of modeling tool, create a wave effect along banner ends.

What do you do when your happily-ever-after dream starts to turn into a nightmare? If you have a need to vent your rage, nothing could be more satisfying and soothing than hitting or slashing something. So why not take a hack at a symbol of your wedded misery? They always said that revenge should be sweet.

frosty split

stuff you'll need

- ax template
- 2 ft. (0.6 m) length ¼ in. (5 mm) soft copper tubing
- craft and serrated knives
- paintbrushes, including stiff brush
- paper towels, moistened with vodka or lemon extract
- palette and small bowl, for mixing paint
- Styrofoam half-ball or block
- airbrush
- 2 ft. (0.6 m) lengths ⅜ in. (8 mm) and ⅛ in. (3 mm) doweling
- drill
- 12 in. (30 cm) round wooden cake board, ½ in. (1 cm) thick, covered in white self-adhesive shelf paper
- no.6 drywall or wood screw and screwdriver
- 3 thin cake boards
- large piping bag and quick-ice tip
- spatula
- turntable (optional)
- plastic wrap
- rolling pin
- rotary cutter
- pliers
- plastic wrap and cardboard, to shield from spatter

food stuff you'll need

- 1 lb. (450 g) modeling chocolate (see page 10)
- airbrush colors: warm brown, ivory, black, and super red
- silver luster dust
- vodka or lemon extract
- 3 x recipe cake batter of choice (see page 11), baked in an 8 in. (20 cm), a 6 in. (15 cm), and a 4 in. (10 cm) round pan
- 4½ cups (1 liter) decorator's buttercream icing (see page 10)
- 4 lb. (1.8 kg) white fondant
- white opaque gel color

1 form the ax
Following template, bend length of copper tubing into ax shape. Leave about 8 in. (20 cm) tubing extending from ax handle. Form ax by molding modeling chocolate around copper shape, guided by template. Round ax handle. Flatten blade edge and bevel with craft knife. Trim as necessary.

2 detail ax handle
Etch woodgrain pattern into handle with craft knife. Brush warm brown airbrush color onto one side of handle, allowing color to settle into etched marks. Wipe away excess with moistened paper towel. Let dry. Repeat for other side of handle.

3 paint the ax head
Mix silver luster dust to a thick paint with a few drops of vodka or lemon extract. Use to paint one side of ax head. Let dry. Turn ax over and paint other side of ax head.

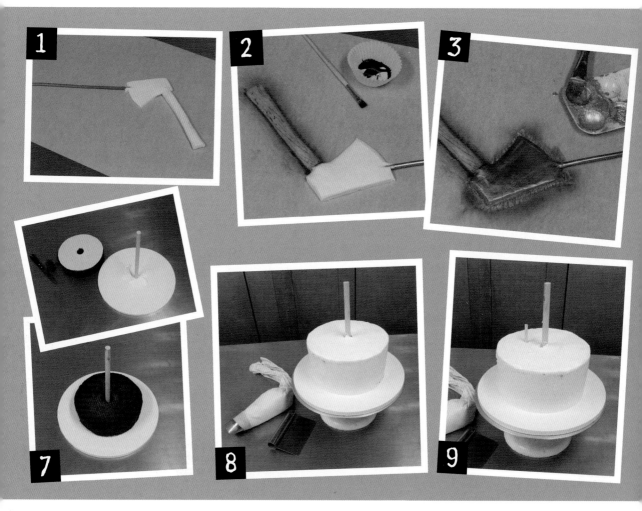

7 position base cake
Cut cakes in half, horizontally. Place 8 in. (20 cm) cake layer onto cake board circle. Core cake to match hole in board. Fix onto doweled cake board with buttercream. Spread buttercream on top. Core second 8 in. (20 cm) cake layer and stack.

8 ice base cake
Using large piping bag and quick-ice tip, pipe buttercream icing over entire surface of cake. Smooth icing with spatula, held at 90° angle to cake edge, turning cake by hand or on a turntable, if you have one.

9 add supporting dowels
Insert four ⅛ in. (3 mm) doweling lengths, arranged in area around the large central dowel, into the top of the iced cake.

4 airbrush the ax

Push end of copper tubing extended from ax head into Styrofoam half-ball or block to support ax. Airbrush light coat of ivory over ax handle to even out color and add shadows. Spray light coat of black over edges of handle and ax head to create shadows. Leave to dry.

5 prepare the board

Cut a 10 in. (25 cm) length of ⅜ in. (8 mm) doweling. Drill pilot hole into center of covered wooden cake board. Drill pilot hole in end of doweling. Attach doweling to cake board with no.6 wood screw.

6 cut cake supports

Cut out 4, 6, and 8 in. (10, 15, and 20 cm) diameter circles from thin cake boards. Cut small hole in center of each to accommodate center-dowel support. Cut eight pieces of ⅛ in. (3 mm) doweling, each as long as height of uncut cakes.

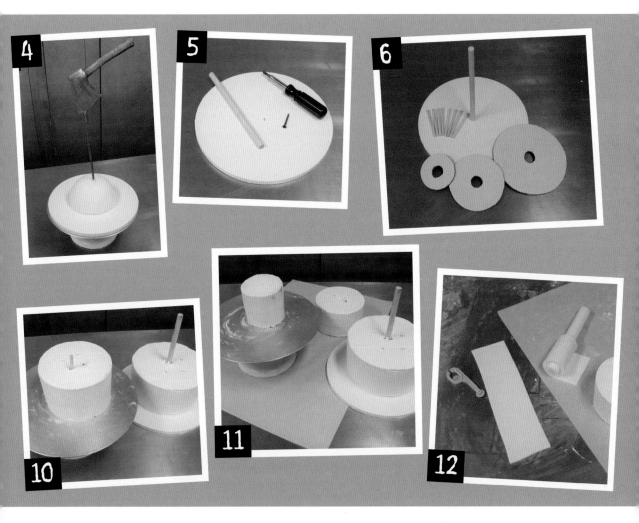

10 ice other cakes

Repeat for 6 in. (15 cm) and 4 in. (10 cm) cake layers, placing on cake board circles, coring centers, sandwiching together, and icing. Insert four ⅛ in. (3 mm) doweling lengths into top of 6 in. (15 cm) cake, arranged around center hole.

11 prepare to add fondant

Set iced cakes aside in a cool place. Do not stack at this stage. Measure the height and circumference of each cake. Roll out half the white fondant onto a dusted surface.

12 add fondant sides

Use rotary cutter to cut out fondant strip, sized to height and circumference of 8 in. (20 cm) cake. Roll over rolling pin and unfurl and smooth onto cake sides. Trim and secure ends with water. Repeat for 6 in. (15 cm) and 4 in. (10 cm) cakes.

13 moisten cake tops

Using a stiff brush, flick and spread a light coating of water over the iced top of each cake. Apply just enough water to soften the surface of the icing a little. Take care not to oversaturate icing.

14 cut fondant tops

Roll out remaining white fondant. Using the 8 in. (20 cm), 6 in. (15 cm) and 4 in. (10 cm) cake pans or cutters as templates, cut out three fondant circles. Cut small center circle in 8 in. (20 cm) and 6 in. (15 cm) pieces to accommodate center dowel.

15 fit fondant tops

Wrap 8 in. (20 cm) fondant circle loosely around rolling pin and unfurl carefully onto moistened top of 8 in. (20 cm) cake. Repeat for 6 in. (15 cm) and 4 in. (10 cm) cakes.

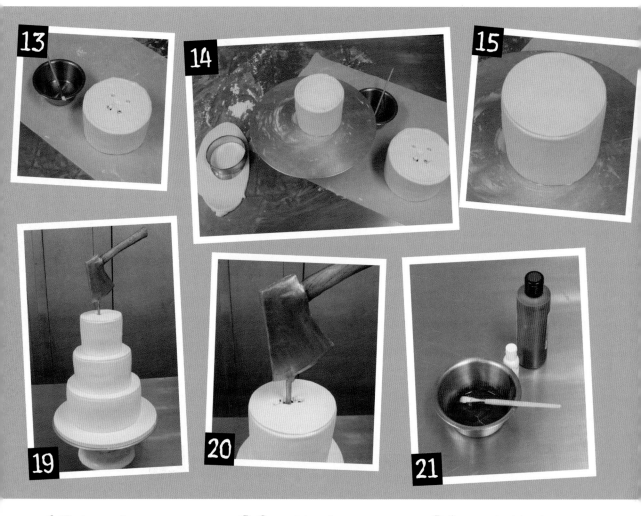

19 insert the ax

Carefully slide the length of copper tubing extending from the ax blade into the top of stacked 4 in. (10 cm) cake. If necessary, use pliers to gently guide the ax into cake.

20 position the ax

For that "just-hacked" look, continue to push the ax down until it appears to be slightly embedded in the top of the cake. If the fondant is too firm, trim a little away to accommodate the ax head.

21 mix the blood

Combine super red airbrush color and white opaque gel color in small bowl. Mix until fully blended. The mixture should have a slightly creamy consistency.

16 smooth fondant

Using your hands, carefully smooth over the fondant on the sides and tops to fix firmly to the iced cakes. Trim and round off edges, moistening slightly if necessary.

17 prepare to stack

Using the large piping bag and quick-ice tip, apply a few dabs of buttercream to top of 8 in. (20 cm) cake.

18 stack the cakes

Carefully stack the fondant-covered 6 in. (15 cm) cake on top of the 8 in. (20 cm) cake. Dab top of 6 in. (15 cm) cake with buttercream. Stack fondant-covered 4 in. (10 cm) cake on top of 6 in. (15 cm) layer.

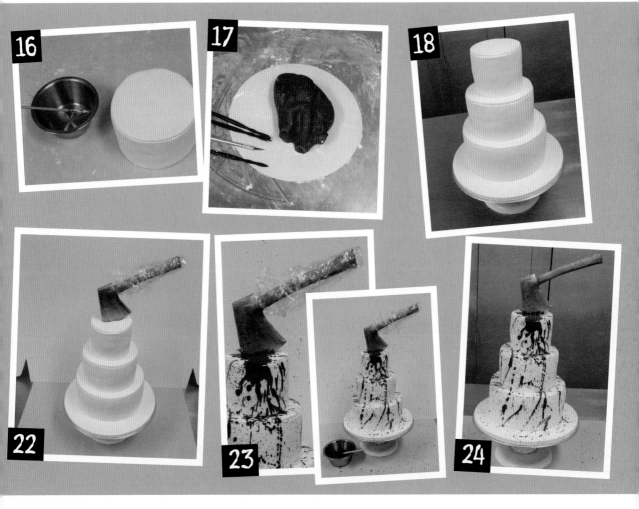

22 prepare spatter area

Place cake onto upturned cake pan or a turntable. Cover the ax handle with plastic wrap to protect it from spatter. Secure a piece of cardboard or paper on the wall behind the cake to protect room from spatter.

23 spatter the cake

Dip stiff, dry paintbrush into blood mixture. With flinging motion, spatter blood onto cake. Turn cake around to spatter on all sides. Repeat until desired effect is achieved. Drip blood from brush in a pool around ax blade.

24 remove the wrap

Carefully remove plastic wrap from ax handle. If you need to store cake, fully cover ax in plastic wrap before placing in a refrigerator, as moisture from condensation will cause paint on modeling chocolate to bead.

Index

Resources

Baking and decorating supplies: confectioneryhouse.com, caljavaonline.com, flourconfections.ca
Airbrushes and compressors: iwata-medea.com
Stripe stencil for Day of the Dead (see pages 24-27): stencilplanet.com
Other: amazon.com

Acknowledgments

Fil Rouge Press would like to thank Gaye Allen for the design and styling of this book, Bruce Fleming for the photography of the finished cakes, Chris Hirneisen for supplying the step photography and templates, Cécile Landau for editing, and Jenny Latham and Julia Halford for additional editorial support.

Color templates

To use the templates below, you will need a printer that you use for edible printing purposes only. Scan the templates on your printer, then print them out on edible printing paper using edible printing ink. Some professional bakeries also offer this service.

Color reference for Lively Candy
(see pages 74-77)

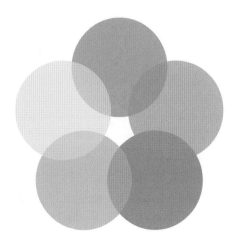

Color reference for Baked Graffiti
(see pages 98-101)

The templates

You will find all the templates in the pocket inside the back cover. The sheets are printed on both sides, so photocopy the templates and laminate your copies for reuse.